MY FA...

FILL IN YOU...

MY NAME IS...

MY FAVOURITE FOOTBALL TEAM IS...

MY FAVOURITE ENGLAND PLAYER IS...

THE POSITION I PLAY IN IS...

THE TEAMS I PLAY FOR ARE...

MY FAVOURITE FOOTBALL BOOTS ARE...

CHECK OUT THESE OTHER MATCH! TITLES FROM MACMILLAN!

MATCH! INCREDIBLE STATS & FACTS

MATCH! JOKE BOOK

MATCH! BUILD YOUR OWN CLUB

MATCH! ANNUAL

TO ORDER, GO TO: WWW.PANMACMILLAN.COM

MATCH!

ENGLAND Football HEROES!

MACMILLAN CHILDREN'S BOOKS

First published 2018 by Macmillan Children's Books
an imprint of Pan Macmillan
20 New Wharf Road, London N1 9RR
Associated companies throughout the world
www.panmacmillan.com

ISBN 978- 1-5290-1403-7

1 3 5 7 9 8 6 4 2

- A CIP catalogue record for this book
is available from the British Library.

Written by Tim O'Sullivan
Edited by Jared Tinslay
Designed by Darryl Tooth
Caps and goals correct up to September 7, 2018.

Printed and bound by CPI Group (UK) Ltd, Croydon CRO 4YY

CONTENTS!

ENGLAND'S WORLD CUP SUPERSTARS PART 1

ENGLAND'S WORLD CUP JOURNEY

ENGLAND'S WORLD CUP SUPERSTARS PART 2

ENGLAND QUIZ 1

ENGLAND'S ALL-TIME LEGENDS

ENGLAND'S GREATEST EVER MOMENTS

ENGLAND QUIZ 2

FIFA U-20 WORLD CUP KOREA REPUBLIC 2017

England's
WORLD CUP
Superstars

5 Reasons Why We Love...

GARETH
SOUTHGATE!

England gaffer Gareth Southgate became a national hero at Russia 2018! Check out five reasons why he's awesome!

1

THE PLAYERS LOVE HIM!

We've never seen players happier to play for The Three Lions. They work hard, but also have fun, which is mainly down to Southgate's relaxed man-management style. Top stuff!

HIS TACTICS RULE!

It was so awesome to see England using a new formation at the World Cup in Russia. Southgate's modern 3-5-2 mixes energetic wing-backs and ball-playing centre-backs, to make a quality playing style!

2

3

HE PICKS ON FORM!

Some previous England managers have picked the same players every year, but he's rewarded stars like Ashley Young and Kieran Trippier for their red-hot PL form!

4

YOUNG STARS GET A CHANCE!

It would've been easy for Southgate to stick with more experienced players, but he decided to give young stars like Jordan Pickford, Jesse Lingard and Marcus Rashford the chance to shine!

HE LOVES ENGLAND!

Southgate won 57 caps for England during his playing career. He bounced back from missing a famous penalty against Germany in the Euro 96 semi-final to manage his country 20 years later!

5

JORDAN PICKFORD

Goalkeeper

Club: Everton	**England Squad Number:** 1
DOB: 07/03/1994	**England Debut:** 10/11/2017
Place of Birth: Washington	**England Caps:** 10
Transfer Value: £40 million	**England Goals:** 0
Strongest Foot: Left	**Top Skill:** Shot-stopping

Jordan Pickford became a real national hero after a sensational summer with The Three Lions! His heroics helped England beat Colombia in the Last 16 to win their first ever penalty shootout at a World Cup. He also pulled off some top-quality saves against Croatia, Belgium and Sweden to silence the questions about who should be England's first-choice goalkeeper. Pickford spent most of his career at his boyhood club Sunderland, before earning a big £30 million move to Everton in 2017. The Toffees struggled in 2017-18, but the shot-stopper still had an epic season and won three prizes at the club's end-of-season awards. The top talent picked up Player Of The Season, Players' Player Of The Season and Young Player Of The Season. We reckon he could be England's No.1 goalkeeper for the next 12 years – he deserves the chance, at least!

HIS GAME RATED!

 His shot-stopping from long range efforts is out of this world!

 He makes himself big for one-on-ones, which is tough for attackers!

✗ *He's still young, so he needs more top-level football to progress!*

PLAYER STATS

REFLEXES
85

SHOT-STOP
95

AGILITY
87

CATCHING
76

KICKING
84

PEN. SAVES
86

STAT ATTACK!

DID YOU KNOW?

Pickford's £30 million move to Everton makes him the sixth most expensive keeper in history!

17

The Everton hero made 17 saves at the 2018 World Cup, and 76% of his goal kicks successfully reached a team-mate!

50

He won 50 caps at youth level for England, playing for six different age groups. 14 of those 50 youth appearances came for the Under-21 side!

Pickford bagged ten clean sheets in the Premier League in 2017-18. He also made 121 saves!

10

1998

Pickford became the first England goalkeeper to save a penalty at the World Cup since 1998, when he stopped Carlos Bacca's spot-kick against Colombia!

England Present

KYLE WALKER

Right/Centre-Back

Club: Man. City	**England Squad Number:** 2
DOB: 28/05/1990	**England Debut:** 12/11/2011
Place of Birth: Sheffield	**England Caps:** 40
Transfer Value: £60 million	**England Goals:** 0
Strongest Foot: Right	**Top Skill:** Lightning pace

England have one of the best full-backs in world footy and his name is Kyle Walker. Like many stars in the current England squad, the Three Lions speedster started his career at Sheffield United and had a ton of the biggest PL clubs scouting him. Tottenham won the race to sign him in 2009, and he quickly proved he was worth the hype with a series of ace all-action performances. His game reached new levels in 2011-12, and he hit the headlines with an incredible goal against Arsenal in the North London derby. His game improved every year and he became one of Spurs' star players, before moving to Man. City for a big fee in 2017. He won the Premier League title in his first season with Guardiola's team, then proved his versatility in a centre-back role for England at the World Cup. Walker is one of Europe's best all-round defenders and could still get even better!

HIS GAME RATED!

 His electric pace and raw strength make him the ultimate defender!

 Walker's fitness levels are incredible. He's up and down the wing!

 He gets in loads of good positions, so should try to score more goals!

PLAYER STATS

PACE
93

POWER
91

SHOOTING
57

DEFENDING
88

HEADERS
83

SKILL
78

DID YOU KNOW?
Walker has been named in the PFA Team Of The Year three times!

STAT ATTACK!

175

He made 175 recoveries in 32 Premier League matches last season. He also played 2,362 passes and made 67 clearances!

24

Walker had bagged 24 assists and five goals in his Premier League career by the end of 2017-18. Awesome!

31

The Man. City ace made 31 clearances during the 2018 World Cup. He also covered 50.2km at the tournament!

2

He'd never won a major trophy in his career before 2018, then won two in three months with the EFL Cup and Premier League for Man. City!

2012

Walker won the PFA Young Player Of The Year award in 2011-12 after a sensational season with Tottenham!

England
Present

DANNY ROSE

Left-Back

Club: Tottenham	**England Squad Number:** 3
DOB: 02/07/1990	**England Debut:** 26/03/2016
Place of Birth: Doncaster	**England Caps:** 23
Transfer Value: £25 million	**England Goals:** 0
Strongest Foot: Left	**Top Skill:** Speedy runs

Energetic and athletic, Danny Rose is a key member of England's hard-working squad! Rose started his career with his local side Leeds, before earning a massive move to Tottenham in 2007. He was sent out on loan four times in the early stages of his Spurs career, and it was his final spell at Sunderland that convinced the North London club to consider him a first-team regular. Since 2013-14, Rose has gone from strength to strength and become one of Europe's best left-backs. He's been linked with moves to Barcelona, Real Madrid and Man. United after showcasing an ace level of form which saw him named in the PFA Team Of The Year for two seasons in a row between 2015-16 and 2016-17. Injuries have slowed him down, but he has the class, confidence, power, attacking talent and the tackling skills to become England's main left-back again very soon!

HIS GAME RATED!

 Danny Rose is brilliant at one-on-one battles with the trickiest wingers!

 He loves getting involved in attacks and has some top crossing skills!

 His injury battles have stopped him reaching world-class level!

PLAYER STATS

PACE
84

POWER
83

SHOOTING
64

DEFENDING
84

HEADERS
74

SKILL
75

DID YOU KNOW?

Rose was named as Sunderland's Young Player Of The Season in 2012-13!

STAT ATTACK!

Rose won 29 caps for England's Under-21 team before breaking into the senior squad in 2016!

29

2016

The Tottenham left-back made his England debut back in 2016, in a 3-2 friendly win against rivals Germany!

By the end of the 2017-18 season, Rose had bagged 14 assists in 145 Premier League matches. He'd also busted nine Prem nets. Wicked!

14

203

Rose played 203 minutes of action for England at the 2018 World Cup. He ran 22.9km and made 80 passes. Awesome!

ERIC DIER

Central Midfielder

Club: Tottenham	**England Squad Number:** 4
DOB: 15/01/1994	**England Debut:** 13/11/2015
Place of Birth: Cheltenham	**England Caps:** 32
Transfer Value: £35 million	**England Goals:** 3
Strongest Foot: Right	**Top Skill:** Versatility

An unselfish team player, Eric Dier is one of the most versatile and reliable members of Gareth Southgate's squad. Dier made his England debut back in 2015 and has been a regular ever since. He became an instant fan favourite in his first year with The Three Lions after bagging a header in a friendly win against Germany, then netting England's first goal of Euro 2016 with an awesome free-kick against Russia! He's also been a star at club level, with a series of consistent performances at centre-back and in midfield for Tottenham. He's had quite a unique career compared to most England stars, because he spent most of his youth career at Portuguese club Sporting, before moving back to England with Spurs in 2014. His intelligent football brain, dominant tackling and willingness to move around the pitch will help protect The Three Lions for years to come!

HIS GAME RATED!

 Dier reads the game brilliantly and never panics in possession!

 He has great technique, which helps with passing and taking free-kicks!

 He's got the ability to control matches, but has to offer himself more!

PLAYER STATS

PACE
66

POWER
85

SHOOTING
63

DEFENDING
81

HEADERS
83

SKILL
71

DID YOU KNOW?
Dier was born in England but grew up in Portugal, and lived there for 13 years!

STAT ATTACK!

33.5

He ran 33.5km in just 248 minutes of action for England during the 2018 World Cup. He also completed 174 passes. Perfect team player!

He's played loads of youth footy for England. He won nine Under-21 caps, six Under-20 caps, eight Under-19 caps and one Under-18 cap!

82

He made 82 clearances for Tottenham in the Premier League last season. He also won 163 of his duels, made 48 interceptions and bagged two assists!

Eric Dier became the first player in history to score a winning spot-kick for England in a World Cup penalty shootout! His strike against Colombia will be remembered forever!

1,059

Dier played 1,059 minutes of action during the 2018 World Cup qualifiers. He also scored one goal and completed 89% of his passes. That's class!

JOHN STONES

Centre-Back

Club: Man. City	**England Squad Number:** 5
DOB: 28/05/1994	**England Debut:** 30/05/2014
Place of Birth: Barnsley	**England Caps:** 33
Transfer Value: £65 million	**England Goals:** 2
Strongest Foot: Right	**Top Skill:** Footy brain

John Stones had a great World Cup at both ends of the pitch! The incredibly classy defender is an ace example of the modern-day centre-back, with technique and decision-making preferred over power and heading ability. This playing style helped him make a real name for himself at Everton, before earning a £50 million move to Man. City. Working under Pep Guardiola and playing Champions League football has taken Stones' game to the next level, which he proved with a series of excellent performances at the World Cup. He was rock-solid at the back all summer, but also chipped in with a shock double against Panama in the group stages! He's only going to get even more experience and confidence at the highest level, and that should help him become one of the planet's best in his position. John Stones can do it all and looks set to keep improving!

HIS GAME RATED!

 His positioning is top class and he reads the game really well!

 Not many centre-backs at international level can pass the ball like Stones!

 His mega confidence can sometimes lead to silly mistakes!

PLAYER STATS

PACE
68

POWER
77

SHOOTING
57

DEFENDING
83

HEADERS
76

SKILL
76

STAT ATTACK!

474

Stones made 474 passes at WC 2018 and completed 456 of them – a 96% pass success rate. What an absolute baller!

He won three trophies in 2018! Bagging a Prem winners' medal was the main prize, but he also won the EFL Cup and Community Shield with Man. City. Get in!

3

73%

The Man. City star had a 73% tackle success rate in the Prem last season. He also made 61 accurate long balls!

Stones scored two goals at the World Cup from six attempts on goal! Nobody expected him to bag a brace against Panama!

2

HARRY MAGUIRE

Centre-Back

Club: Leicester

DOB: 05/03/1993

Place of Birth: Sheffield

Transfer Value: £60 million

Strongest Foot: Right

England Squad Number: 6

England Debut: 08/10/2017

England Caps: 12

England Goals: 1

Top Skill: Heading

Harry Maguire is a superstar in England after some outrageously good displays at the 2018 World Cup. Footy fans up and down the country fell in love with his epic no-nonsense playing style, crazy Hulk-like strength and awesome headers. He started his career at boyhood club Sheffield United, but really made a name for himself at Hull. Leicester loved his all-action performances for The Tigers and paid £17 million to sign him in June 2017. He made his England debut just four months later, then went on to feature for The Three Lions at the 2018 World Cup. His super defending rocked Russia all summer, but his greatest moment arrived against Sweden in the quarter-finals. Maguire powered in an unstoppable header to give England a 1-0 lead and help them reach their first World Cup semi-final for 28 years. Because of that, the CB became a hero everywhere!

HIS GAME RATED!

 Maguire leaps like a basketball star to win loads of headers!

 He's an excellent passer and his accuracy helps start attacks, too!

 His lack of pace can be a weakness against really quick forwards!

PLAYER STATS

PACE
61

POWER
91

SHOOTING
58

DEFENDING
86

HEADERS
94

SKILL
71

DID YOU KNOW?

Maguire is a massive Sheffield United fan and still tries to see some games!

STAT ATTACK!

1

Maguire's goal against Sweden in the World Cup quarter-finals was his first for England. It came on his tenth cap for The Three Lions!

The Leicester centre-back had a 73% tackle success rate during the 2017-18 Premier League season. He also made 115 headed clearances for The Foxes!

73

645

The England hero played a total of 645 minutes at the 2018 World Cup. He ran 65.1km, completed 380 passes and recovered the ball 50 times. Hero!

Harry made his England debut in October 2017. He played the full 90 minutes as England beat Lithuania 1-0 in a World Cup qualifier!

Maguire's header against Sweden was England's first goal in a World Cup quarter-final since Michael Owen opened the scoring v Brazil at the 2002 World Cup!

2002

England Present

JESSE LINGARD

Attacking Midfielder

Club: Man. United	**England Squad Number:** 7
DOB: 15/12/1992	**England Debut:** 08/10/2016
Place of Birth: Warrington	**England Caps:** 18
Transfer Value: £40 million	**England Goals:** 2
Strongest Foot: Right	**Top Skill:** Long shots

Jesse Lingard is a fan favourite for his LOL Instagram posts and crazy celebrations, but he proved at Russia 2018 that his main skill is being awesome at footy! Lingard played most of his youth football at Man. United and possessed the talent to break into the first team at Old Trafford. Jesse started to show off his natural ability on the biggest stage in 2015-16 and had a massive moment at the end of that season, scoring the winner against Crystal Palace in the FA Cup final after coming on as a sub. He continued to learn and develop the following season, catching the eye of new England boss Gareth Southgate. Lingard soon became a regular for The Three Lions and Southgate's faith was paid off. He had an awesome World Cup, hitting an unforgettable strike against Panama. He curled the ball into the top corner beautifully to show off his super talent to the world!

HIS GAME RATED!

 He gets loads of chances by making really clever runs into the box!

 Lingard is excellent at shooting from outside the box! He's so lethal!

❌ *He can get knocked off the ball too easily by defenders sometimes!*

PLAYER STATS

PACE
81

POWER
59

SHOOTING
74

DEFENDING
65

HEADERS
69

SKILL
87

MATCH! 37

STAT ATTACK!

2016

The Man. United ace is the last English player to score in an FA Cup final, after netting in 2016!

J-Lingz has won four different trophies during his professional career with Man. United, including the EFL Cup and the Europa League in 2017!

4

17

Lingard had 17 attempts on goal during the 2018 World Cup. He also ran 67.8km at the tourno and completed a whopping 93% of his passes!

DID YOU KNOW?

J-Lingz helped Man. United to the FA Youth Cup in 2010-11. Hero!

8

He bagged eight goals and five assists in the Prem last season. He also made 932 passes and hit the woodwork three times. Unlucky!

JORDAN HENDERSON

Central Midfielder

Club: Liverpool	**England Squad Number:** 8
DOB: 17/06/1990	**England Debut:** 17/11/2010
Place of Birth: Sunderland	**England Caps:** 44
Transfer Value: £30 million	**England Goals:** 0
Strongest Foot: Right	**Top Skill:** Stamina

Jordan Henderson has been playing for The Three Lions for eight years, but 2018 was the year he truly established himself as an England superstar. Helping Liverpool reach the Champions League final improved Hendo's game management skills, footy brain and confidence, which made him a really important player on England boss Gareth Southgate's teamsheet. The all-action hero was a machine for The Reds in the Champo League against Roma and Man. City, and he brought that big-game form to Russia for The Three Lions. His career began at boyhood club Sunderland, but he completed a move to Liverpool for a big fee in 2011. He didn't make an instant impact, but improved every year and eventually earned the captain's armband! He's shown he can be a true leader for both his club and country, and that will continue for many years to come!

HIS GAME RATED!

 Hendo fights for every ball and plays with incredible passion!

 He has mind-blowing fitness levels! The CM never stops running!

 His shooting needs to improve to be the complete midfielder!

PLAYER STATS

PACE
71

POWER
76

SHOOTING
62

DEFENDING
85

HEADERS
75

SKILL
72

DID YOU KNOW?

Henderson won the Prem Goal Of The Month award in September 2016, for his awesome strike against Chelsea!

STAT ATTACK!

57.1
Hendo ran 57.1km during the World Cup in Russia! His epic energy and fitness levels helped The Three Lions dominate midfield in games!

Jordan won 27 caps for the England Under-21 team before breaking into the senior squad!

2012
He reached two cup finals in his first season with Liverpool. He lost the 2012 FA Cup final, but won the League Cup against Cardiff!

The Liverpool midfielder won 51 tackles in the Premier League in 2017-18! He also made a massive 213 recoveries and won 98 duels!

1,347
The England hero played a mega total of 1,347 minutes during England's 2018 World Cup qualifying campaign!

HARRY KANE

Striker

Club: Tottenham

DOB: 28/07/1993

Place of Birth: London

Transfer Value: £150 million

Strongest Foot: Right

England Squad Number: 9

England Debut: 27/03/2015

England Caps: 30

England Goals: 19

Top Skill: Finishing

Tottenham's Harry Kane is one of the world's greatest strikers and already an England legend! He was a real breakout star in the Premier League in 2014-15 and quickly earned his first England call-up. He didn't disappoint – he scored just a minute and a half into his debut against Lithuania, becoming a Three Lions regular ever since and going to WC 2018 as captain. Kane proved he was worth the armband by winning the Golden Boot in his first ever World Cup tournament, and by becoming the first England player to win the net-busting prize since Gary Lineker in 1986. As well as netting six times, he was also a real leader throughout the tourno. He's always linked with a mega move to the likes of Real Madrid and Man. United, but he's ready to take Tottenham and England to the next level. You're looking at a future legend of the game!

HIS GAME RATED!

 He's one of the greatest finishers in the history of the Premier League!

 Kane's strength and hold-up play are too much for defenders!

 He's not the quickest player, but he doesn't normally need pace!

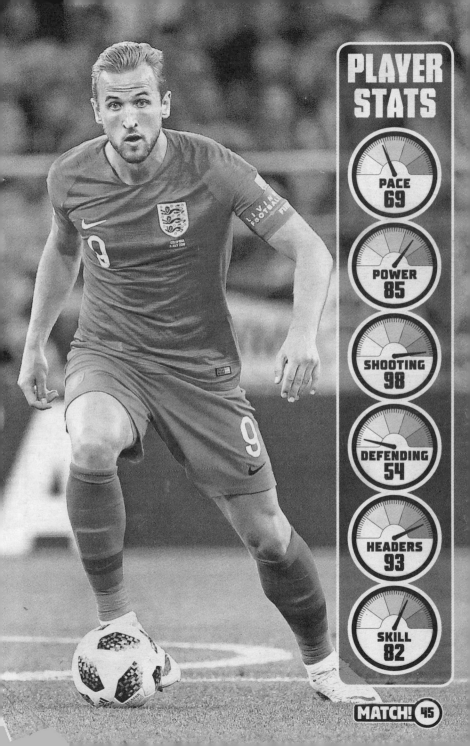

PLAYER STATS

PACE
69

POWER
85

SHOOTING
98

DEFENDING
54

HEADERS
93

SKILL
82

MATCH! 45

STAT ATTACK!

14

The England hero had 14 shots during the World Cup. Seven were off target, one was blocked and the other six went in. Hero!

Kane's treble v Panama saw him become just the third English player to bag a hat-trick at a World Cup!

3

105

Harry scored 105 Premier League goals in the four seasons between 2014-15 and 2017-18. Most strikers would take that total for their whole career!

Kane has finished first, first and second in the last three Prem Golden Boot charts. His finishing is just off the scale!

2

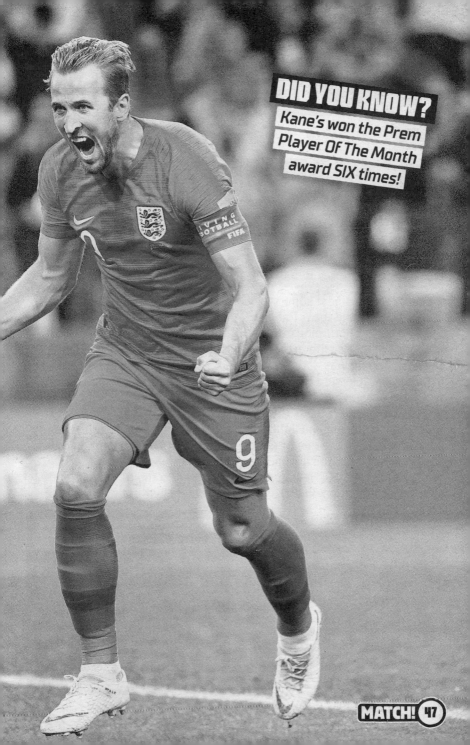

RAHEEM STERLING

Forward

Club: Man. City	**England Squad Number:** 10
DOB: 08/12/1994	**England Debut:** 14/11/2012
Place of Birth: Kingston	**England Caps:** 44
Transfer Value: £65 million	**England Goals:** 2
Strongest Foot: Right	**Top Skill:** Speedy dribbling

One of the flashiest superstars in this sick England team, Raheem Sterling is rapidly turning into one of world football's elite attacking talents. Sterling was actually born in Jamaica, but moved to England when he was young and earned a spot in QPR's youth team. It was his electric dribbling and lightning pace that caught the eye of many scouts, which resulted in a move to Liverpool in 2010. He improved every year from then on, becoming a household name in 2013-14 after a jaw-dropping season with The Reds. His wicked link-up play in attack with Luis Suarez, Daniel Sturridge and Steven Gerrard saw Liverpool finish second in the Prem, and his red-hot form didn't go unnoticed – Man. City bought him a year later for nearly £50 million! Under Pep Guardiola and Gareth Southgate, Sterling has gone to the next level and will surely just get even better!

HIS GAME RATED!

 His movement is just incredible, which gives him loads of chances!

 Not many forwards at international level have his pacy dribbling skills!

 His one-on-one finishing can sometimes be poor. He should score more!

PLAYER STATS

PACE
95

POWER
59

SHOOTING
70

DEFENDING
51

HEADERS
65

SKILL
90

DID YOU KNOW?

Raheem Sterling won Europe's Golden Boy award in 2014 – a prize previously won by Lionel Messi and Sergio Aguero!

STAT ATTACK!

18 Sterling grabbed 18 goals and 11 assists in the Premier League in 2017-18! He was a major part of Man. City's title success!

He had ten shots on goal during the 2018 World Cup! He also went on 16 dribbles – more than any other England player – and completed eight of them!  **10**

192 Sterling had played 192 Premier League games by the end of the 2017-18 season. He'd notched 49 goals and 33 assists in that time!

The Man. City speed machine bagged three assists in 1,049 minutes of action during England's qualifying campaign for World Cup 2018!  **3**

 **34.97** Sterling hit a top speed of 34.97km/h last season. That's absolutely rapid!

JAMIE VARDY

Striker

Club: Leicester	**England Squad Number:** 11
DOB: 11/01/1987	**England Debut:** 07/06/2015
Place of Birth: Sheffield	**England Caps:** 26
Transfer Value: £35 million	**England Goals:** 7
Strongest Foot: Right	**Top Skill:** Electric pace

Jamie Vardy has had one of the coolest careers in football history. He was playing non-league footy most of his career, then bagged a move to Leicester in 2012 and rapidly turned into a world-class striker. It's like something from a Hollywood movie, but it happened in real life and he became a really important member of England's squad. After helping Fleetwood win promotion to League Two in 2011-12, Vardy joined The Foxes and started an epic journey which resulted in Leicester winning the Premier League title in 2015-16. It was the most incredible title victory in footy history and Vardy was the most talked-about footy hero in the UK. His sensational work-rate, aggressive playing style and electric pace are tough to stop for any defender on the planet – as he proved at the start of the 2018-19 PL season with a goal v Man. United at Old Trafford!

HIS GAME RATED!

 He fights for every ball and runs his socks off in every match!

 Vardy is devastating on the counter-attack with his rapid pace!

 He sometimes struggles if opponents play deep and defensive!

PLAYER STATS

PACE
92

POWER
86

SHOOTING
85

DEFENDING
64

HEADERS
72

SKILL
76

20

Jamie Vardy finished fourth in the Prem scoring charts last season. He scored 20 league goals, including doubles against Arsenal and Tottenham!

STAT ATTACK!

392

Vardy played 392 minutes for England during the 2018 World Cup qualifiers. He scored two goals and had a 44% shot accuracy!

Vardy netted 24 goals in just 36 games as Leicester shocked the world and won the Premier League title in 2015-16!

24

157

The England hero ran 19.3km in just 157 minutes of action during the 2018 World Cup. His fitness and passion are off the scale!

WORLD CUP 2018

Journey

England had a summer they'll never forget! MATCH looks at their seven matches at the 2018 World Cup!

GAME	DATE	STAGE	STADIUM	ATTENDANCE
1	18/06/2018	Group G	Volgograd Arena	41,064

 TUNISIA **1-2** **ENGLAND**

Sassi 35 (p) Kane 11, 90+1

England kicked off World Cup 2018 in dramatic style with a stoppage-time win against Tunisia. The Three Lions played some of the best footy England fans have seen since Euro 2004 in the first half, with the rapid pace of Jesse Lingard and Raheem Sterling causing all sorts of problems! It looked like it would be a frustrating draw, but Harry Kane's back-post header in the 91st minute gave England three points to kick off an epic summer!

ENGLAND'S MAN OF THE MATCH
Harry Kane

All eyes were on new England captain Harry Kane before the tourno started, and he proved he was worth the hype with a lethal double in The Three Lions' first match! England really needed to start with a win, so Kane was key!

MATCH STATS

TUNISIA		ENGLAND
41%	% Possession	59%
1	Shots on target	7
3	Shots off target	7
2	Corners	7
2	Offsides	3

MATCH RATING
★ ★ ★ ★

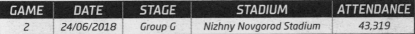

GAME	DATE	STAGE	STADIUM	ATTENDANCE
2	24/06/2018	Group G	Nizhny Novgorod Stadium	43,319

ENGLAND 6-1 PANAMA

Stones 8, 40; Kane 22 (p), 45 (p), 62; Lingard 36   *Baloy 78*

England made it two wins out of two with a devastating 6-1 victory over Panama. Harry Kane proved he's one of the best penalty takers in the world with two unstoppable spot-kicks in the first half. He completed his hat-trick by deflecting a shot into the net in the second half, but he wasn't the only goal king that day. Man. City centre-back John Stones got in on the act with a shock double, while Jesse Lingard scored a cracking curled shot!

ENGLAND'S MAN OF THE MATCH
Jesse Lingard

Jesse Lingard didn't net as many goals as Harry Kane or John Stones in this match, but he had an incredible game! As well as scoring a sizzling goal, the Man. United hero showed off some class skills and bundles of energy all match!

MATCH STATS

England		Panama
58%	% Possession	42%
7	Shots on target	2
3	Shots off target	5
3	Corners	2
3	Offsides	0

MATCH RATING
★ ★ ★ ★

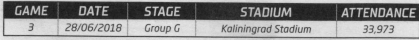

ENGLAND **0-1** **BELGIUM**

Januzaj 51

England's first defeat at the World Cup arrived in the final game of Group G against Belgium. Both teams had already qualified for the Last 16, so the atmosphere and energy wasn't the same as in the previous games.

The match looked like it was heading for a boring 0-0 snooze-fest, before former Man. United winger Adnan Januzaj curled an unstoppable effort past Jordan Pickford to give Belgium a narrow group-winning 1-0 victory!

ENGLAND'S MAN OF THE MATCH

Trent Alexander-Arnold

On a difficult night for England, Alexander-Arnold made the most of his opportunity in Southgate's starting line-up with a really sick performance. His work-rate, pace, energy and intensity ruled - his potential is amazing!

MATCH STATS

England		Belgium
48%	% Possession	52%
1	Shots on target	4
7	Shots off target	4
7	Corners	2
3	Offsides	1

MATCH RATING

★

GAME	DATE	STAGE	STADIUM	ATTENDANCE
4	03/07/2018	Last 16	Spartak Stadium	44,190

COLOMBIA 1-1 ENGLAND

Mina 90+3   AET   Kane 57 (p)

England win 4–3 on pens

This was the moment that England fans up and down the country started going crazy, because The Three Lions had finally won a penalty shootout! England had lost their previous three World Cup shootouts, but now it was their turn for some spot-kick glory. Colombia equalised in stoppage time with a real sucker punch, then went ahead in the shootout, but heroics from the agile Jordan Pickford and Eric Dier sealed a famous victory!

ENGLAND'S MAN OF THE MATCH
Jordan Pickford

Keeper Jordan Pickford silenced his critics and became an overnight superstar after this performance against Colombia. His epic save from Mateus Uribe and then the penalty stop from Carlos Bacca will always be remembered!

MATCH STATS

Colombia		England
49%	% Possession	51%
4	Shots on target	2
7	Shots off target	9
2	Corners	7
1	Offsides	2

MATCH RATING
★ ★ ★ ★

GAME	DATE	STAGE	STADIUM	ATTENDANCE
5	07/07/2018	Quarter-Final	Samara Arena	39,991

 SWEDEN **0-2** **ENGLAND**

Maguire 30, Alli 59

England had been exciting to watch uner Gareth Southgate, but this was the game the whole world respected them as a really professional, classy and serious international team. The pressure was on The Three Lions to reach their first World Cup semi-final since 1990, but they didn't show any nerves and dominated the game from start to finish. Excellent headers from Leicester ace Harry Maguire and Spurs hero Dele Alli sealed the boys a win!

ENGLAND'S MAN OF THE MATCH
Harry Maguire

Leicester powerhouse Harry Maguire became a total fan favourite with an ace all-action performance against Sweden. His powerful header gave England their opener, and his defending was rock-solid the whole game!

MATCH STATS

Sweden		England
43%	% Possession	57%
3	Shots on target	2
3	Shots off target	4
1	Corners	6
2	Offsides	1

MATCH RATING
★ ★ ★ ★

 CROATIA **2-1** **ENGLAND**

Perisic 68, Mandzukic 109 **AET** Trippier 5

England's wicked World Cup adventure came to an end in the Russian capital, after a really dramatic semi-final with Croatia. The Three Lions were just 22 minutes away from the WC final after Tottenham right-back Kieran Trippier put them into an early lead with an incredible free-kick, but Southgate's men couldn't hold on, and Perisic's clever 68th minute finish made it 1-1. Mario Mandzukic won it for Croatia in extra-time with a left-footed strike!

ENGLAND'S MAN OF THE MATCH

Kieran Trippier

Kieran Trippier had a brilliant tournament, but his best moment arrived in this semi-final. He gave England the lead with a perfect free-kick into the top corner, showcasing his wicked technique and top-quality confidence!

MATCH STATS

Croatia		England
54%	% Possession	46%
7	Shots on target	1
11	Shots off target	6
8	Corners	4
1	Offsides	3

MATCH RATING

★ ★ ★

BELGIUM 2-0 ENGLAND

Meunier 4, E. Hazard 82

England's World Cup campaign ended with a 2-0 defeat to Belgium in the third place play-off. Both teams were struggling to show their normal levels of energy after suffering semi-final heartbreak earlier in the week, but

The Red Devils managed to grab the bronze medal. PSG right-back Thomas Meunier scored really early on for his side, before Eden Hazard made it 2-0 with a smart finish past England and Everton goalkeeper Jordan Pickford!

ENGLAND'S MAN OF THE MATCH
John Stones

The Man. City centre-back had an impressive tournament and ended it in style with a class performance against Belgium. He kept rival Man. United striker Romelu Lukaku quiet all game, but would've loved a clean sheet!

MATCH STATS

Belgium		England
43%	% Possession	57%
4	Shots on target	5
3	Shots off target	7
4	Corners	5
1	Offsides	0

MATCH RATING
★ ★

HARRY KANE

Golden Boot

2018 FIFA World Cup Russia™   adidas

Harry Kane became the first England player to win the World Cup Golden Boot since 1986! Check out his six goals in Russia!

Tunisia **v** England

Goal 1 — Kane tapped in from close range after the keeper parried poorly!

Goal 2 — A class stoppage-time header flew perfectly into the near corner!

England **v** Panama

Goal 3 — He rifled an unstoppable pen past the keeper into the far left corner!

Goal 4 — Another incredible penalty blasted more or less into the same spot!

Goal 5 — A shot deflected off Kane's heel to complete a famous hat-trick!

PREVIOUS WINNERS!

Year	Player	Goals
2018	*Harry Kane, England*	6
2014	*James Rodriguez, Colombia*	6
2010	*Thomas Muller, Germany*	5
2006	*Miroslav Klose, Germany*	5
2002	*Ronaldo, Brazil*	8
1998	*Davor Suker, Croatia*	6
1994	*Hristo Stoichkov, Bulgaria* *Oleg Salenko, Russia*	6
1990	*Salvatore Schillaci, Italy*	6
1986	*Gary Lineker, England*	6

Colombia **v** England

Goal 6 — He kept calm after a long delay to slam a penalty down the middle!

KIERAN TRIPPIER

Right-Back

Club: Tottenham	**England Squad Number:** 12
DOB: 19/09/1990	**England Debut:** 13/06/2017
Place of Birth: Bury	**England Caps:** 13
Transfer Value: £45 million	**England Goals:** 1
Strongest Foot: Right	**Top Skill:** Crossing

Trippier has rapidly turned into one of the world's best full-backs. The 28-year-old defender spent most of 2017-18 wrestling with Serge Aurier for the right-back spot at Tottenham, but England boss Gareth Southgate made him first-choice at the World Cup – and he didn't regret it! Trippier mixed incredible energy and work-rate with awesome technique to be one of the stars of the tourno. He flew up and down the right wing like a cheetah all summer, then stunned the planet with an epic free-kick against Croatia in the semi-final. Tripps started his ace career with Man. City before they were Premier League giants, but couldn't break into the first team, so moved on to Burnley. He made a huge impact at Turf Moor, and earned himself a move to London club Tottenham in 2015 for a fee of around £3.5 million. That's a bargain for one of their key men!

HIS GAME RATED!

 Trippier's awesome pace, work-rate and crossing are his main strengths!

 His technique is out of this world and he can take a mean free-kick!

 He sometimes attacks too much and leaves gaps in defence!

PLAYER STATS

PACE
84

POWER
77

SHOOTING
71

DEFENDING
83

HEADERS
70

SKILL
76

DID YOU KNOW?
Trippier won Burnley's Player Of The Year award in 2011-12!

STAT ATTACK!

1990
Trippier's free-kick against Croatia was England's first goal in a World Cup semi-final since Gary Lineker's dramatic equaliser against West Germany at the 1990 World Cup!

The 28-year-old had bagged 15 assists in just 80 Premier League games by the end of the 2017-18 season. That's an incredible tally for a right-back!

15

328
The Tottenham ace made 328 passes at the 2018 World Cup – 244 of them were successful, including 30 long passes!

Kieran Trippier is one of just three players in history to score for England in a World Cup semi-final. The other two are Bobby Charlton and Gary Lineker! Awesome!

3

580
The Spurs hero played 580 minutes for The Three Lions at the 2018 World Cup. His epic fitness also helped him cover 67.6km during the tournament!

JACK BUTLAND

Goalkeeper

Club: Stoke	**England Squad Number:** 13
DOB: 10/03/1993	**England Debut:** 15/08/2012
Place of Birth: Bristol	**England Caps:** 8
Transfer Value: £20 million	**England Goals:** 0
Strongest Foot: Right	**Top Skill:** Reflexes

Jack Butland is one of the best English shot-stoppers around! His battle with Everton superstar Jordan Pickford for England's number one shirt could've gone either way, because Three Lions manager Gareth Southgate is a massive fan of the Stoke star's epic goalkeeping skills. Butland started his career at Birmingham and eventually became one of The Blues' star players, before getting a move to Stoke in 2013.

After two years of being behind Asmir Begovic in the pecking order, Butland became first choice at the start of the 2015-16 season and never looked back. Injuries slowed him down in 2016-17, but he was back with a bang in 2017-18 with a series of eye-popping performances. He's now bossing it in the Championship following Stoke's relegation, but Butland has the talent to be a Premier League star again!

HIS GAME RATED!

 He oozes confidence and doesn't let big strikers push him around!

 Butland is awesome at saving powerful long-range shots!

 He's sometimes criticised for not coming off his line quick enough!

PLAYER STATS

REFLEXES
84

SHOT-STOP
84

AGILITY
76

CATCHING
78

KICKING
76

PEN. SAVES
69

STAT ATTACK!

2012

He made his England debut all the way back in 2012, in a 2-1 victory over Italy. He was just 19 at the time, and became the youngest keeper ever to represent the senior side!

He won 28 caps for the England Under-21 side and represented The Three Lions at the 2013 UEFA European Under-21 Championship!

28

144

The Stoke hero made a mind-blowing 144 saves in the Premier League last season – more than any other keeper!

DID YOU KNOW?

Butland was named in the Team Of The Tournament at the 2010 UEFA European Under-17 Championship!

Butland has kept 20 clean sheets in just 77 games during his time in the Premier League. They're well impressive stats!

20

England Present

DANNY WELBECK

Forward

Club: Arsenal	**England Squad Number:** 14
DOB: 26/11/1990	**England Debut:** 29/03/2011
Place of Birth: Manchester	**England Caps:** 40
Transfer Value: £15 million	**England Goals:** 16
Strongest Foot: Right	**Top Skill:** Work-rate

Danny Welbeck is a great team player and one of England's most underrated goal kings. Apart from Harry Kane, Welbeck has the best scoring rate in the current squad with 16 goals in just 40 matches. The hard-working forward played most of his career at boyhood club Man. United before moving south to Arsenal in 2014. During his time at Old Trafford, Welbeck won the Premier League title and League Cup. He went on to win the FA Cup with Arsenal in 2017, and became a vital part of The Gunners' squad during Arsene Wenger's final few seasons at The Emirates. Welbeck's unselfish attitude and epic work-rate have made him a favourite of every manager he's worked for! Some critics reckon he needs to score more club goals, but Welbeck gets himself in more goalscoring positions than most forwards because of his great movement!

HIS GAME RATED!

 Welbeck fights for every ball and has incredible work-rate!

 He's not greedy in front of goal and is always looking for team-mates!

 Welbeck isn't a natural finisher and can struggle in one-on-one situations!

PLAYER STATS

PACE
85

POWER
79

SHOOTING
70

DEFENDING
64

HEADERS
69

SKILL
72

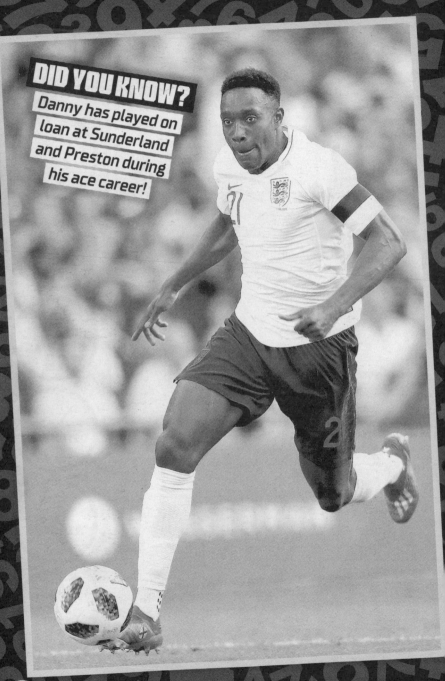

DID YOU KNOW?
Danny has played on loan at Sunderland and Preston during his ace career!

STAT ATTACK!

14

He won 14 caps for England's Under-21 side and also played for the U19s, U18s and U17s!

In 2012-13, Welbeck played 27 games for Man. United to help them win a record 13th Premier League title!

27

198

By the end of the 2017-18 season, Welbeck had scored 41 goals in 198 Premier League games. He had also bagged 19 Prem assists. Get in!

Welbeck has won the Community Shield three times in his career. He lifted the trophy in 2011, 2013 and 2017. Hero!

3

2012

Danny helped England finish top of Group D at Euro 2012 with an incredible backheel goal against Sweden!

GARY CAHILL

Centre-Back

Club: Chelsea	**England Squad Number:** 15
DOB: 19/12/1985	**England Debut:** 03/09/2010
Place of Birth: Dronfield	**England Caps:** 61
Transfer Value: £15 million	**England Goals:** 5
Strongest Foot: Right	**Top Skill:** Marking

Gary Cahill is still going strong after a wicked career at club and international level. He was a fan favourite at Aston Villa and then Bolton in the early stages of his career, thanks to his no-nonsense playing style, but a move to The Blues in 2012 took his game to another level. In fact, it was just four months after leaving The Trotters for Chelsea that Cahill was playing in a Champo League final. The powerful centre-back didn't show any signs of nerves or lack of big-game experience with a commanding performance in club footy's biggest game. He helped The Blues stun Bayern Munich in their own stadium and lifted the famous trophy in his first season with the London club. This helped Cahill become a household name and, of course, an England regular! He's never relied on crazy pace, so the Chelsea hero could stay at the top level for another five years!

HIS GAME RATED!

 Cahill is very consistent and rarely makes big mistakes in games!

✓ *His strength and clever positioning have always been top class!*

 He struggles when fast strikers drag him wide and out of position!

PLAYER STATS

PACE
58

POWER
93

SHOOTING
64

DEFENDING
86

HEADERS
89

SKILL
62

2

Cahill has won the
Premier League title
twice in his career! He
lifted the famous
trophy in 2014-15
and 2016-17!

STAT ATTACK!

27

By the end of the 2017-18 season, Cahill had scored 27 Premier League goals in his career. That's decent for a centre-back!

3

Gary has been named in the PFA Team Of The Year three times in his epic career. The last time was in 2016-17!

90

He only played 90 minutes at the 2018 World Cup, but ran over 10km and completed 96% of his passes. Wicked!

PHIL JONES

Centre-Back

Club: Man. United	**England Squad Number:** 16
DOB: 21/02/1992	**England Debut:** 07/10/2011
Place of Birth: Preston	**England Caps:** 27
Transfer Value: £20 million	**England Goals:** 0
Strongest Foot: Right	**Top Skill:** Blocking

Phil Jones is one of the toughest defenders in the country and has the potential to dominate at the back for years to come. Former Man. United boss Sir Alex Ferguson - one of the greatest managers in football history - once said that Jones could become the best ever player in the Red Devils' famous history. If Fergie is saying that about the CB, he must be a very special talent! He ended the 2010-11 season really strongly for boyhood club Blackburn, which alerted the Premier League's top teams. Man. United decided to sign him and he's been at Old Trafford ever since. The 26-year-old has won five trophies during his time with the Red Devils, including the Prem title in 2012-13. He has the ability to win even more honours in the future and become one of Europe's best centre-backs - his power and aggression are tough to stop when he's on top form!

HIS GAME RATED!

 His passion is incredible - he throws himself in front of everything!

 He barges strikers out of the way with his super strength!

 Many modern defenders are quick, but Jones lacks that electric speed!

PLAYER STATS

PACE
54

POWER
84

SHOOTING
53

DEFENDING
80

HEADERS
86

SKILL
60

MATCH! 81

DID YOU KNOW?

Jones made his England debut in a Euro 2012 qualifier against Montenegro!

STAT ATTACK!

17

He played 17 games during Man. United's last Premier League title-winning season in 2012-13. He made 59 clearances that year!

Man. United kept 15 clean sheets in the 23 Premier League games Jones played last season. He's a rock at the back for United!

15

180

He played 180 minutes of action at the 2018 World Cup in Russia. He ran 19.1km in the two games and completed 95% of passes!

Jones won nine caps for England's Under-21 team before playing for the senior squad. He also played four times for the U19s!

9

450

He played 450 minutes of action and won 67% of his tackles during England's 2018 World Cup qualifying campaign. Sick stats!

FABIAN
DELPH

Central Midfielder

Club: Man. City	**England Squad Number:** 17
DOB: 21/11/1989	**England Debut:** 03/09/2014
Place of Birth: Bradford	**England Caps:** 15
Transfer Value: £25 million	**England Goals:** 0
Strongest Foot: Left	**Top Skill:** Versatility

Fabian Delph is a key member of Gareth Southgate's squad, thanks to his epic consistency, leadership qualities, work-rate and ability to play either in midfield or at the back. The Man. City hero can play as a full-back, central midfielder or even as a winger, and performs at the highest level wherever he is! He was born in Yorkshire and began his professional career with local team Leeds, before wowing scouts around the country and making a big-money move to Prem side Aston Villa in 2009. He had a brilliant career with the Midlands giants and captained Villa in their 2015 FA Cup final loss v Arsenal. Man. City came calling at the start of the 2015-16 season and Delph quickly became one of their most reliable players. He's already won one Premier League title, featuring 22 times for Guardiola's side last season, and his trophy cabinet might need more space soon!

HIS GAME RATED!

 Delph has a top footy brain and tries to keep the ball moving!

 He's incredibly versatile and can play in many different positions!

✗ *He gets rotated a lot at City so doesn't get a good run of games!*

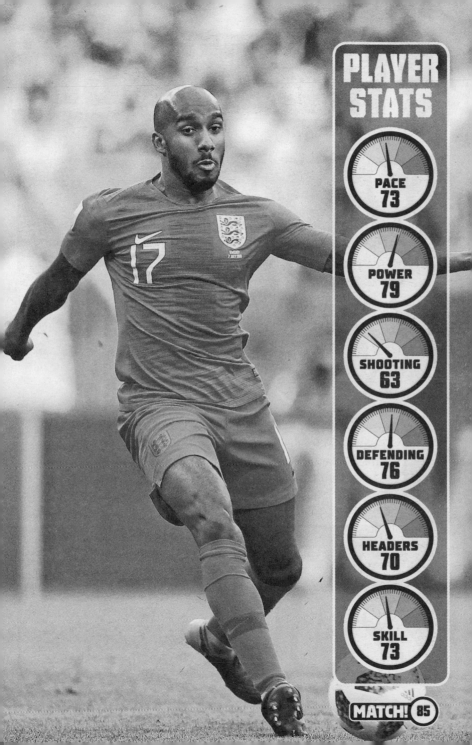

PLAYER STATS

PACE
73

POWER
79

SHOOTING
63

DEFENDING
76

HEADERS
70

SKILL
73

MATCH! 85

STAT ATTACK!

3

Fabian Delph grabbed three Premier League goals and two assists for Aston Villa in the 2013-14 season!

4

Delph won four caps for the England Under-21 team before breaking into the senior squad. He also played twice for the U19s!

220

The Man. City hero played 220 minutes of action at the 2018 World Cup in Russia. He also made 159 passes and completed 89% of them. Pure class!

73

He averaged 73 passes per game in the Prem last season and made 149 recoveries. Epic!

England Present

ASHLEY YOUNG

Left-Back

Club: Man. United	**England Squad Number:** 18
DOB: 09/07/1985	**England Debut:** 16/11/2007
Place of Birth: Stevenage	**England Caps:** 39
Transfer Value: £20 million	**England Goals:** 7
Strongest Foot: Right	**Top Skill:** Work-rate

Most of England's 23-man World Cup squad made their Three Lions debuts in the last few years, but not Ashley Young. He played his first senior international game in 2007! Back then, Young was an exciting left winger, full of tricks and electric pace, but now he's in the squad for his experience, footy brain and set-piece skills. He's totally reinvented himself as a left-back, and still shows bags of energy, passion and skill. After an excellent 2017-18, Young was able to force his way back into the England setup and was eventually named Gareth Southgate's first choice left-back in time for the World Cup. Euro 2020 starts just before his 35th birthday, but don't be surprised if Young's still pulling on the famous white shirt at the next major tournament! Southgate is forming a really exciting young squad, but they still need leaders with experience – just like Young!

HIS GAME RATED!

 His work-rate is unreal. He fights for every ball until the final whistle!

 He's a modern full-back with bundles of energy and great technique!

 He might struggle to keep up with the pace of a rapid winger!

PLAYER STATS

PACE
81

POWER
76

SHOOTING
69

DEFENDING
82

HEADERS
71

SKILL
77

MATCH! **89**

DID YOU KNOW?

Ashley Young won the Premier League Player Of The Month award three times in 2008!

STAT ATTACK!

72

The Man. United left-back made 72 clearances in 30 Prem games last season. He also made 53 tackles and 168 recoveries. What a hero!

Young bagged 23 goals and assists combined for Aston Villa in the 2007-08 Premier League season. Awesome!

23

462

He played 462 minutes of action at the World Cup in Russia. He ran 47.9km in that time and put in 17 crosses!

Young has won five trophies with Man. United, including the Prem title, the FA Cup, the EFL Cup and the Europa League!

5

2009

Young won the PFA Young Player Of The Year award in 2008-09, after an epic season with The Villans!

MARCUS RASHFORD

Striker

Club: Man. United	**England Squad Number:** 19
DOB: 31/10/1997	**England Debut:** 27/05/2016
Place of Birth: Manchester	**England Caps:** 25
Transfer Value: £50 million	**England Goals:** 3
Strongest Foot: Right	**Top Skill:** Acceleration

Marcus Rashford could be the future superstar of this young and exciting England team. He's one of the youngest members of the squad, but it already feels like he's a major part of the team and someone who can cause havoc at major tournaments for years to come. Blessed with sensational pace and a ruthless eye for goal, Rashford burst onto the scene with boyhood club Man. United in 2016 by scoring an incredible double on his Prem debut against Arsenal. He became a household name overnight and ex-England manager Roy Hodgson handed him a shock call-up to The Three Lions' Euro 2016 squad. Rashford was the only real bright spark in England's shock Last 16 defeat to Iceland, even though he came on as a late substitute! His exciting and fearless playing style made him an instant fan favourite, and he could become an England legend!

HIS GAME RATED!

 Rashford can beat any defender on the planet with his electric pace!

He surprises goalkeepers by shooting with power from every angle. Nice!

 His long-range shooting totally rules, but he should improve his one-on-ones!

PLAYER STATS

PACE
94

POWER
66

SHOOTING
84

DEFENDING
52

HEADERS
70

SKILL
80

STAT ATTACK!

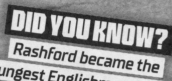

11

Rashford was called up to England's Euro 2016 squad after playing just 11 Premier League games for Man. United. Wow!

6

The Man. United hero went on six dribbles into the box during the 2018 World Cup! He also had five shots from 211 minutes of action!

7

Rashford bagged seven goals and five assists in the PL for United in 2017-18!

He's already lifted four trophies! He won the Community Shield and FA Cup in 2016, then the EFL Cup and Europa League in 2017. Awesome!

4

England Present

DELE ALLI

Attacking Midfielder

Club: Tottenham	**England Squad Number:** 20
DOB: 11/04/1996	**England Debut:** 09/10/2015
Place of Birth: Milton Keynes	**England Caps:** 30
Transfer Value: £55 million	**England Goals:** 3
Strongest Foot: Right	**Top Skill:** Composure

England megastar Dele Alli is already one of the best attacking midfielders in the world! Dele always seems to be in the right place at the right time, because he has the football brain to time his runs into the box perfectly. Once or twice in a season would be luck, but he does it almost every game! He's also one of the best midfielders in world footy at scoring headers – as he proved against Sweden in the World Cup quarter-final and also on the opening weekend of the 2018-19 Premier League season against Newcastle. Born in Milton Keynes, Dele played for his local team until Tottenham signed him in 2015. MK Dons must have wished they got a bigger fee than £5 million, because Alli has gone on to become one of the most exciting players in the Prem and an England regular. He defo has the natural talent and confidence to get even better!

HIS GAME RATED!

✓ *He attacks headers with excellent technique and calm confidence!*

✓ *Dele's movement and runs into the box are world-class!*

✗ *Improving his tackling would make him the perfect midfielder!*

PLAYER STATS

PACE
76

POWER
72

SHOOTING
83

DEFENDING
62

HEADERS
85

SKILL
81

DID YOU KNOW?

Dele was named in the Prem PFA Team Of The Year in 2015–16 and 2016–17!

STAT ATTACK!

117

Dele completed 117 passes for England at the 2018 World Cup. He played 364 minutes of action and covered over 46km!

The Tottenham ace bagged two goals and two assists during England's 2018 World Cup qualifying campaign!

2

17

He won 17 caps for England's youth teams, featuring for the U17s, U18s, U19s and U21s!

Dele scored a Prem double three games in a row between December 2016 and January 2017, which included two against Chelsea!

3

1990

His class header v Sweden in the quarter-final helped England reach their first World Cup semi-final since 1990. Absolute legend!

RUBEN LOFTUS-CHEEK

Central Midfielder

Club: Chelsea	**England Squad Number:** 21
DOB: 23/01/1996	**England Debut:** 10/11/2017
Place of Birth: London	**England Caps:** 8
Transfer Value: £30 million	**England Goals:** 0
Strongest Foot: Right	**Top Skill:** Ball control

Ruben Loftus-Cheek earned a call-up to Gareth Southgate's 2018 World Cup squad after a top-quality season on loan at Crystal Palace. The Chelsea CM mixes incredible power and pure athleticism with jaw-dropping technique to make the ultimate central midfield powerhouse. He grew up with Chelsea's youth team and was handed a place in the senior squad, but couldn't break into the starting line-up and had to eventually move out on loan to Palace for first-team football. RLC was on fire from minute one of his time with The Eagles, and his red-hot form bagged him his first England cap in a friendly against Germany in November 2017. He was named Man Of The Match on his debut and instantly became a massive part of The Three Lions' squad. He's back at Chelsea now, and ready to hit the big time – as long as he's given the game time!

HIS GAME RATED!

 He holds up the ball with incredible strength and has class control!

 Loftus-Cheek has a great range of short and long distance passing!

✗ *He needs to improve his shooting to become the complete midfielder!*

PACE
78

POWER
95

SHOOTING
61

DEFENDING
76

HEADERS
80

SKILL
79

DID YOU KNOW?
RLC bagged 17 caps for the England U21s and scored seven goals!

STAT ATTACK!

6

He made six Premier League appearances for Chelsea during their title-winning season in 2016-17!

2

Loftus-Cheek bagged two Prem goals and three assists while on loan at Palace in 2017-18!

723

RLC played over 700 passes for Crystal Palace in the Prem last season. He also won 188 duels and made 22 interceptions!

4

Loftus-Cheek played four games for England at the 2018 World Cup. He made a real impact, going on seven dribbles into the penalty area. Big threat!

TRENT ALEXANDER-ARNOLD

Right-Back

Club: Liverpool	**England Squad Number:** 22
DOB: 07/10/1998	**England Debut:** 07/06/2018
Place of Birth: Liverpool	**England Caps:** 2
Transfer Value: £35 million	**England Goals:** 0
Strongest Foot: Right	**Top Skill:** Surging runs

Trent Alexander-Arnold has all the talent to be a future England legend, and maybe one of the best full-backs on the planet! Liverpool were struggling with right-back options in 2017-18 due to injury problems, but Alexander-Arnold stepped forward to take control of the situation. We've seen tons of examples in the past when a reserve player takes the place of an injured star, then goes back to the bench when the first-choice player comes out of the physio room. But that hasn't happened with TAA. The young defender showcased an incredible mix of athleticism and tackling skills in 2017-18, and could now be The Reds' main right-back for the next 15 years! His awesome displays in the Champo League knockout stages proved he could perform in the biggest games, and that was the reason he was fast-tracked into England's World Cup squad!

HIS GAME RATED!

 He reads the game so well for someone with so little experience!

 His pace and athleticism help him make loads of recovery tackles!

 He's not as powerful as some full-backs, but that should defo improve!

PLAYER STATS

PACE
87

POWER
68

SHOOTING
60

DEFENDING
78

HEADERS
70

SKILL
72

DID YOU KNOW?

TAA hit 102 crosses for Liverpool in the Prem last season!

STAT ATTACK!

2

Alexander-Arnold won Liverpool's Young Player Of The Season award in both 2016-17 and 2017-18. Sick!

11

TAA bagged 11 caps for the England Under-17 team. He also won ten caps for the U19s and three for the U21s!

39

He made 39 clearances in just 19 PL games last season. He also played over 1,000 passes - averaging 53 per game!

7

The wonderkid made his England debut in a WC warm-up friendly v Costa Rica on June 7, 2018!

79

Trent only played 79 minutes of action during the World Cup. Those minutes came in the third group game against Belgium!

NICK POPE

Goalkeeper

Club: Burnley	**England Squad Number:** 23
DOB: 19/04/1992	**England Debut:** 07/06/2018
Place of Birth: Soham	**England Caps:** 1
Transfer Value: £25 million	**England Goals:** 0
Strongest Foot: Right	**Top Skill:** Catching

There weren't many footy fans who knew much about Nick Pope before the 2017-18 season, but he quickly turned himself into a household name. Burnley thought they were in terrible trouble when Tom Heaton picked up a serious shoulder injury last September, but Pope proved he had the quality to become The Clarets' number one with a series of top performances. His superb positioning, athleticism and shot-stopping skills helped his side finish seventh in the Premier League table. He kept 11 clean sheets in 35 league appearances, then earned a deserved call-up to England's 2018 World Cup squad! Pope spent his youth career at Ipswich, before bagging his first professional contract with Bury. He moved to Charlton in 2011 and spent a lot of his time out on loan, before eventually joining Burnley in 2016 and becoming one of the best Premier League goalkeepers!

HIS GAME RATED!

 He has incredible bravery and reflexes in one-on-one situations!

 Pope is confident with his feet and can pass the ball out from the back!

 He still needs more experience at the top level in the big games!

PLAYER STATS

REFLEXES
83

SHOT-STOP
82

AGILITY
80

CATCHING
84

KICKING
77

PEN. SAVES
72

STAT ATTACK!

1,099

The England ace made 1,099 passes in the Prem in 2017-18, including 362 accurate long balls. He's just as good with his feet as he is with his hands!

During his time at Charlton, Pope was sent out on loan to six different clubs in just four years. How mad is that?

6

114

Pope made 114 saves in the Premier League in 2017-18 and kept 11 clean sheets. He was a real beast between the sticks for Burnley!

DID YOU KNOW?
Pope was named Burnley's Player Of The Year in 2017-18!

1

Pope pulled off one penalty save in the Prem in 2017-18. He easily kept out Joselu from the spot in January to earn his side a valuable point!

ANAGRAMS!

Rearrange the letters to find the England heroes!

1. RYNKA HERA

2. EARSNE MHGIRTLE

3. KECO IPNP

4. LSNAO EGYYHU

5. DYNOE NRAS

SOCCER SCRAMBLE

Use the remaining letters to discover an England legend!

S₁ R₁ R₁
A₁ E₁ E₁
V₄ G₂
T₁

| | | E | | N |
| | | R | | D |

ACTION REPLAY ◀◀

How much do you remember about England's mega World Cup semi-final against Croatia?

1 Which Man. City star picked up The Three Lions' only yellow card of the game?

2 Who scored a free-kick to put England 1-0 up?

3 Which Serie A winger equalised for Croatia?

4 Which ace central midfielder was named in the first XI – Eric Dier or Jordan Henderson?

5 Who scored Croatia's winning goal in the 109th minute?

QUIZ 1 ANSWERS!

ANAGRAMS!

1. Harry Kane
2. Raheem Sterling
3. Nick Pope
4. Ashley Young
5. Danny Rose

ACTION REPLAY!

1. Kyle Walker
2. Kieran Trippier
3. Ivan Perisic
4. Jordan Henderson
5. Mario Mandzukic

SOCCER SCRAMBLE!

Steven Gerrard

116 MATCH!

England's **ALL-TIME** *Legends*

BOBBY MOORE

Centre-Back

DOB: 12/04/1941	**England Caps:** 108
Place of Birth: Barking	**England Goals:** 2
Strongest Foot: Right	**Top Skill:** Tackling
Main Club: West Ham	**Played like...** Raphael Varane

Bobby Moore is a footy legend and will be remembered forever as the captain of England's 1966 World Cup winning team! He was a born leader on and off the pitch, but also an extraordinary defender. He brought the ball out from the back before it became part of the modern game and had sensational technique for a centre-back. He had an awesome battle with iconic Brazil striker Pele at the 1970 WC, and the pair swapped shirts after the game as a sign of respect for each other. Moore spent most of his club career at boyhood team West Ham, and The Hammers retired Moore's number six shirt in 2008 so no future players would ever wear it. On top of that, Moore was honoured with his own statue outside Wembley Stadium, proving how much of a legend he is! Footy has seen loads of great defenders over the years, but Moore was on another level. He played with an incredible controlled aggression, always took fair play seriously and put his team-mates above himself. Bobby Moore, a footballing legend!

HIS GAME RATED!

 Moore was famous for his incredible reading of the game!

 His tackling technique was class. He always took the ball cleanly!

 His international career was ace, but he could've won more at club level!

PLAYER STATS

PACE
77

POWER
92

SHOOTING
53

DEFENDING
99

HEADERS
95

SKILL
83

DID YOU KNOW?

The ace defender was named West Ham's Player Of The Year four times!

STAT ATTACK!

1994

Moore was named in the FIFA World Cup All-Time Team in 1994!

He's the one and only England man to ever lift the World Cup as captain. He was the star in 1966!

1

647

Moore played 647 games for West Ham between 1958 and 1974. He's third on the list of all-time appearance makers for The Hammers. Awesome!

He won two major trophies during his epic career with West Ham – the FA Cup in 1963-64 and the UEFA Cup Winners' Cup in 1964-65!

2

1970

The West Ham legend came really close to winning the Ballon d'Or. He finished second in the 1970 vote!

WAYNE ROONEY

Striker

DOB: 24/10/1985	**England Caps:** 119
Place of Birth: Liverpool	**England Goals:** 53
Strongest Foot: Right	**Top Skill:** Technique
Main Club: Man. United	**Played like...** Roberto Firmino

Wayne Rooney is The Three Lions' all-time record goalscorer! He's also the second most-capped man in England history, just six behind keeper Peter Shilton, so there's no argument that he's a proper England legend! Rooney's finest moment with The Three Lions arguably arrived at the start of his international footy career, with three incredible displays at Euro 2004. Injury forced him to be subbed in the quarter-final against Portugal, but he'd already made a massive impact by then.

Wazza started the tournament with an absolutely awesome performance against France in the first group game, before stunning Switzerland with an unstoppable double. He saved the best for last with two more awesome goals in the final group stage game against Croatia! He'd become the latest superstar of European footy, and everyone was talking about him. It was a really special tourno for Wazza, but becoming the nation's all-time top scorer just about trumps it!

HIS GAME RATED!

 Rooney played every England game with intense passion!

 His technique was so good. He could shoot from anywhere!

 He didn't always bring his Man. United form to the England team!

PLAYER STATS

PACE
73

POWER
97

SHOOTING
94

DEFENDING
67

HEADERS
86

SKILL
87

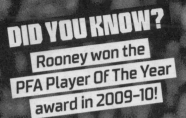

5

He won five Premier League titles with Man. United in his ace career, including three in a row between 2006-07 and 2008-09!

STAT ATTACK!

Wazza scored 208 goals in 491 games during his awesome Premier League career. He's the second top scorer in Prem history behind Alan Shearer!

208

53

He's England's all-time top goalscorer with 53 goals. He's also the most capped outfield player in history with 119 appearances!

2004

Wayne Rooney was given the Golden Boy award in 2004 - a year before it was won by Barcelona star Leo Messi!

GEOFF HURST

Striker

DOB: 08/12/1941	**England Caps:** 49
Place of Birth: Ashton	**England Goals:** 24
Strongest Foot: Right	**Top Skill:** Finishing
Main Club: West Ham	**Played like...** Gonzalo Higuain

Sir Geoff Hurst must have been stopped in the street thousands of times in his life, because he was the man who won the World Cup for England with a stunning hat-trick against West Germany in the 1966 final! He was on fire the whole game and leaped brilliantly for England's first goal, meeting a stunning cross with a beautiful header into the corner. The Three Lions thought they'd won it after Martin Peters scored in the 78th minute, but West Germany scored a late equaliser to make it 2-2 after 90 minutes. Up stepped Hurst in extra-time as he put England 3-2 up with a smart turn and finish – the ball cracked the bar and landed over the line. Then he completed his hat-trick at the end of extra-time with a superb counter-attack goal, finished by Hurst smashing the ball into the top corner. He nearly didn't play the World Cup final after star striker Jimmy Greaves recovered from injury, but Hurst kept his place in the starting line-up and the rest is history. What an absolute hero!

HIS GAME RATED!

 Hurst had ace movement in the 18-yard box. He was so intelligent!

 He could finish brilliantly with both feet without losing shot power!

✗ *He could have score more – he won fewer caps than other England top scorers!*

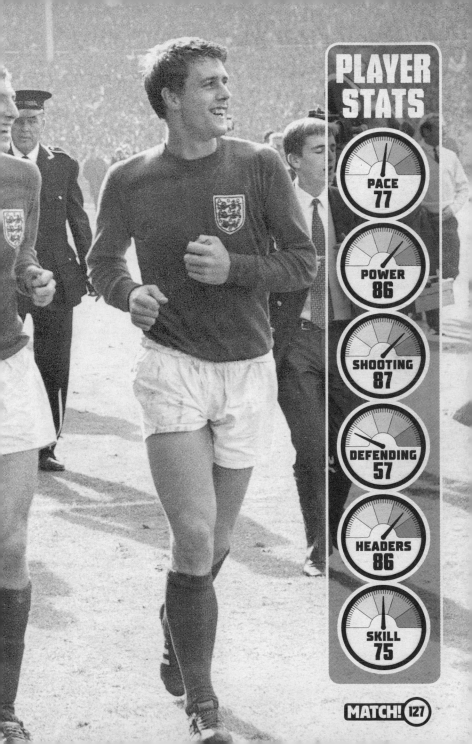

PLAYER STATS

PACE
77

POWER
86

SHOOTING
87

DEFENDING
57

HEADERS
86

SKILL
75

DID YOU KNOW?

Hurst scored during West Ham's 3–2 win v Preston in the 1964 FA Cup Final!

STAT ATTACK!

4 Hurst played football in four different countries during his epic career, finishing in the United States with Seattle Sounders!

He played the whole 90 minutes as West Ham beat 1860 Munich in the 1965 UEFA European Cup Winners' Cup final. Awesome!

90

249 The England icon is the second top goalscorer in West Ham's famous history. Hurst bagged 249 goals for The Hammers!

Hurst is the only football star in history to score a hat-trick in a World Cup final. His treble against West Germany is absolutely legendary!

3

1966 Hurst didn't just rip up the final at the 1966 World Cup. The England legend also scored the only goal in a 1-0 victory over Argentina in the quarter-final. Legend!

England Legends

GARY LINEKER

Striker

DOB: 30/11/1960	**England Caps:** 80
Place of Birth: Leicester	**England Goals:** 48
Strongest Foot: Right	**Top Skill:** Finishing
Main Club: Leicester	**Played like...** Jermain Defoe

You might see Gary Lineker on TV and think he's always been a footy presenter, but the truth is he became famous for being a red-hot striker! Lineker busted loads of nets for his local team Leicester, before earning a big move to Everton in 1985. They were one of the best teams in Europe at the time! He had a jaw-dropping season with The Toffees, then won the Golden Boot at the 1986 World Cup in Mexico, which alerted La Liga giants Barcelona. Lineker spent three seasons at the Nou Camp, before returning to England with Tottenham and winning the FA Cup in 1991. England fans love him because he scored when it really mattered – at the major tournaments! Lineker had a quiet time at Euro 88, then exploded into life when England needed him the most at World Cup 1990. He scored a match-winning brace against Cameroon in the quarter-finals, then netted an equaliser against West Germany in the semis to finish on four goals!

HIS GAME RATED!

 Lineker was the best at sniffing out chances with his wicked movement!

 He had a lethal right foot and would rarely miss when through on goal!

 He struggled with aerial duels against taller and tougher defenders!

PACE
74

POWER
66

SHOOTING
88

DEFENDING
51

HEADERS
79

SKILL
67

DID YOU KNOW?
Lineker finished second in the Ballon d'Or vote in 1986!

STAT ATTACK!

1990

Lineker received a FIFA Fair Play award in 1990 for never picking up a red or yellow card in his career!

He fluffed the chance to equal Bobby Charlton's previous record of 49 England goals by missing a pen against Brazil!

49

3

He was the English First Division top scorer three times, which is like winning the Premier League Golden Boot in modern football!

The England legend won the PFA Player Of The Year award during his one and only season with Everton in 1985-86!

1

MICHAEL OWEN

Striker

DOB: 14/12/1979

Place of Birth: Chester

Strongest Foot: Right

Main Club: Liverpool

England Caps: 89

England Goals: 40

Top Skill: One-on-ones

Played like... Sergio Aguero

Michael Owen is one of the best strikers in England's long history! Only injuries stopped him from being England's all-time record goalscorer, because his pace and finishing skills were unstoppable. He exploded onto the scene with Liverpool in 1997, scoring on his debut against Wimbledon, and electrified fans with his incredible pace. He caught the eye of former England boss Glenn Hoddle, who fast-tracked Owen into the squad for the 1998 World Cup, and what happened next would change the striker's life forever. He came on as a substitute to score a brilliant equaliser against Romania in the group stages, then started the Last 16 clash against Argentina and stunned everyone with one of the best goals in World Cup history. He ran from the centre circle and dribbled past loads of Argentina players, before striking the ball with perfection into the top corner of the net. He went on to star at the 2002 WC and Euro 2004 in a glittering career which also saw him play for Real Madrid!

HIS GAME RATED!

 Owen's pace at the start of his career had to be seen to be believed!

 He was absolutely lethal in one-on-one situations with the goalkeeper!

 Injuries really affected his performances in the latter part of his career!

PLAYER STATS

PACE
96

POWER
61

SHOOTING
93

DEFENDING
51

HEADERS
70

SKILL
86

DID YOU KNOW?

The England legend won the FA Cup, League Cup and UEFA Cup with Liverpool back in 2000-01!

STAT ATTACK!

Owen won the Sports Personality Of The Year award in 1998!

He scored a legendary hat-trick in England's iconic 5-1 win away to Germany in a 2002 WC qualifier!

He scored 150 goals in just 326 games during his Premier League career. That put him eighth in the all-time scoring charts at the start of the 2018-19 season. Machine!

Owen won back-to-back Premier League Golden Boots in 1997-98 and 1998-99! He also won the PL title with Man. United in 2010-11!

Owen became the first English player to win the Ballon d'Or since 1979, when he picked up the famous prize in 2001!

BOBBY CHARLTON

Attacking Midfielder

DOB: 11/10/1937

Place of Birth: Ashington

Strongest Foot: Right

Main Club: Man. United

England Caps: 106

England Goals: 49

Top Skill: Long shots

Played like... Paul Pogba

Sir Bobby Charlton was England's top scorer for nearly 50 years, before Wayne Rooney broke the record in 2015. Charlton's long-standing record was even more impressive because he wasn't even a forward and still scored nearly one goal every two games. Full of pace, power, work-rate, creativity and a dynamite long shot, Charlton is regarded as one of footy's greatest ever players. His best moment in an England shirt came in the 1966 World Cup semi-final against Portugal. The Three Lions were 90 minutes away from their first ever World Cup final and Charlton stepped up with the best performance of his career. He scored both goals in a 2-1 win, including a missile shot from just inside the 18-yard box! Charlton enjoyed his greatest footy moment with England at Wembley in 1966, but was also part of the famous 'Busby Babes' Man. United squad and helped The Red Devils lift their first ever European Cup in 1968 as captain. He was the ultimate midfielder!

HIS GAME RATED!

 Charlton's long shots were full of power and brilliant accuracy!

 Opponents just couldn't handle his mega powerful runs through midfield!

 He could've won even more trophies in his epic football career!

PLAYER STATS

PACE
85

POWER
86

SHOOTING
93

DEFENDING
58

HEADERS
83

SKILL
92

STAT ATTACK!

1966

Charlton won the Ballon d'Or and Golden Ball in 1966 for his incredible performances at the World Cup for England!

2

Charlton scored two goals as United won their first European Cup in a 4-1 win against Benfica in 1968!

1963

He played the full 90 mins as Man. United won the 1963 FA Cup final against Leicester!

3

He won three First Division titles during his time at Man. United, which is what the main English championship was called before the Premier League came along!

DAVID BECKHAM

Right Winger

DOB: 02/05/1975	**England Caps:** 115
Place of Birth: Leytonstone	**England Goals:** 17
Strongest Foot: Right	**Top Skill:** Crossing
Main Club: Man. United	**Played like...** Kevin De Bruyne

David Beckham is an England legend and arguably the most famous football star in history! Becks eventually became more popular for his celebrity status off the pitch, but nobody should forget what made him such a massive global icon in the first place – his wicked footy skills! Legendary Man. United boss Sir Alex Ferguson replaced older stars for players from the youth team in 1995-96 and Beckham was one of his wonderkids. By the start of 1996-97, Beckham was a first-team regular and had been given the famous No.10 shirt. He sent shockwaves through the Prem by scoring from the halfway line in the first game of the season against Wimbledon. For The Three Lions, he recovered from a really controversial red card v Argentina at the 1998 World Cup to become the captain for years! Perhaps his greatest moment for England came against Greece in 2001 – The Three Lions were losing 2-1, but Becks' injury-time free-kick sent them to the 2002 World Cup. Total hero!

HIS GAME RATED!

 Beckham is arguably the best crosser of the ball in English football history!

 His free-kick technique rocked. He regularly found the top corner!

 His technique and footy brain made up for his total lack of speed!

PLAYER STATS

PACE
67

POWER
71

SHOOTING
74

DEFENDING
69

HEADERS
61

SKILL
95

STAT ATTACK!

Becks played 265 Prem matches for Man. United. He bagged 62 goals and 80 assists in that time!

Beckham was part of Man. United's famous treble-winning team from 1998-99, helping his side win the PL, FA Cup and Champions League!

Beckham won 115 caps for England, which puts him third in the all-time list of appearances for the men's senior team!

He won eight European league titles in his epic career, including six Prem trophies with United, one La Liga for Real Madrid and Ligue 1 with PSG!

Becks won the Sports Personality Of The Year award in 2001 after his last-second free-kick against Greece helped England qualify for the 2002 World Cup. Legend!

PETER SHILTON

Goalkeeper

DOB: 18/09/1949	**England Caps:** 125
Place of Birth: Leicester	**England Goals:** 0
Strongest Foot: Right	**Top Skill:** Reflexes
Main Club: Nott'm Forest	**Played like...** Thibaut Courtois

Peter Shilton is easily one of the greatest keepers in football history – and England's all-time record appearance maker. He won an incredible 125 caps for The Three Lions, which is six more than nearest challenger Wayne Rooney. Shilton started his epic professional career the same year that England won the World Cup, in 1966 with local team Leicester. He stayed there until 1974 and made over 300 appearances, but eventually joined Stoke. His top performances for The Potters caught the eye of Nottingham Forest, who snapped him up in 1977. What followed was the peak of his great career, with a First Division title in 1978, then back-to-back European Cups in 1979 and 1980. Those trophies are known as the Premier League and Champions League nowadays, so it proves how good he was. He also starred for The Three Lions at the 1986 and 1990 World Cups, and former managers and football experts reckon he was basically unbeatable when on top form!

HIS GAME RATED!

 Shilton was the world's best shot-stopper in the late 1970s!

✓ *He commanded his box with great power and catching technique!*

 For such an awesome shot-stopper, he wasn't great at penalty saves!

PLAYER STATS

REFLEXES
93

SHOT-STOP
94

AGILITY
85

CATCHING
92

KICKING
79

PEN. SAVES
72

STAT ATTACK!

DID YOU KNOW?
Shilton won Southampton's Player Of The Season award in 1984-85 and 1985-86!

2

He played at two World Cup tournaments for England. Shilton was the goalkeeper when Diego Maradona scored the famous 'Hand Of God' goal in 1986!

10

He was named in the PFA Team Of The Year ten times! That's five times more than current Man. United GK David de Gea!

2

Shilton helped Forest shock Europe and win two European Cup trophies in 1979 and 1980!

1990

Shilton won the last of his 125 England caps in The Three Lions' third place play-off against Italy at the 1990 World Cup!

PAUL GASCOIGNE

Attacking Midfielder

DOB: 27/05/1967	**England Caps:** 57
Place of Birth: Gateshead	**England Goals:** 10
Strongest Foot: Right	**Top Skill:** Dribbling
Main Club: Tottenham	**Played like...** Philippe Coutinho

Paul 'Gazza' Gascoigne is one of the most popular footy stars in history! He became a legend with England fans for pulling silly faces and his cheeky personality, but it was mainly down to him being an awesome footballer. His dribbling and passing skills were on another level to most players. If you've never seen Gazza play, you need to check out some YouTube clips, because he had some eye-popping tekkers! England had a good team going into the 1990 World Cup, but Gazza gave them the X-factor to make them great. His vision and dribbling were exactly what The Three Lions needed to get over the horror show of Euro 88 when they failed to even get a point. He was a major reason why England reached the semis in 1990, with sick individual displays against The Netherlands and Cameroon! He won the hearts of the nation in the dramatic semi-final against West Germany, because he picked up a yellow card and started crying on the pitch. He would've missed the final if England had got there!

HIS GAME RATED!

 Gazza could beat anyone with his dribbling and total close control!

 His crossing skills and free-kick accuracy were incredible!

 Gazza sometimes picked up too many silly yellow and red cards!

PLAYER STATS

PACE
82

POWER
78

SHOOTING
79

DEFENDING
55

HEADERS
66

SKILL
97

DID YOU KNOW?
Gazza won the Sports Personality Of The Year award in 1990!

STAT ATTACK!

1985

Gazza started his professional career at Newcastle in 1985 and played 92 league games for his boyhood club. Local hero!

Gascoigne was named in the PFA Team Of The Year in 1987-88 and 1990-91. He also won the PFA Young Player Of The Year prize in 1987-88!

1991

He scored a memorable 35-yard free-kick for Tottenham against local rivals Arsenal in the 1991 FA Cup semi-final. Unstoppable!

He played for nine clubs during his career, including a surprise move to Italian giants Lazio and a three-year spell with Rangers in Scotland!

1996

Gascoigne's most famous goal was at Euro 96 for England v Scotland. He flicked the ball over Colin Hendry's head, then volleyed past Andy Goram!

ASHLEY COLE

Left-Back

DOB: 20/12/1980	**England Caps:** 107
Place of Birth: London	**England Goals:** 0
Strongest Foot: Left	**Top Skill:** Driving runs
Main Clubs: Arsenal & Chelsea	**Played like...** Marcelo

Ashley Cole is one of the best ever full-backs in footy history. England's displays have been up and down over the last 20 years, but Cole was one of the only consistently world-class players during that time. Former England boss Sven-Goran Eriksson handed Cole a shock call-up in 2001 when he was just 20 years old, and he kept the country's left-back spot for the next 12 years! Before Cole made such a massive impact in club and international footy, full-backs were all about defending. But he changed all that and started a new wave of attacking, all-action and athletic full-backs. He was an epic tackler, but also joined in attacks with electric pace, awesome team play and superb crossing tekkers! Cole also had a wicked club career. He was part of Arsenal's famous unbeaten season in 2003-04, then went on to win the Champions League and Europa League with Chelsea. Cole completely changed how full-backs played the game and will go down in history as an all-time great of English football!

HIS GAME RATED!

 Cole's footy brain was awesome. He rarely made a mistake!

 He'd run up and down the left wing all game. So much energy!

 He never scored for The Three Lions, but netted 15 Premier League goals!

PLAYER STATS

PACE
86

POWER
79

SHOOTING
62

DEFENDING
95

HEADERS
80

SKILL
82

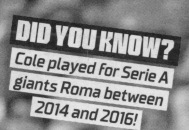

DID YOU KNOW?

Cole played for Serie A giants Roma between 2014 and 2016!

7

He's won more FA Cup trophies than any player in history! Cole bagged seven winners' medals, including three for Arsenal and four for Chelsea. Total legend!

STAT ATTACK!

2004

Ashley Cole was a massive part of the famous Arsenal team that went unbeaten in the 2003-04 Premier League season. Ledge!

Cole played at five major tournos for England, including Euro 2004, where he received massive praise for brilliantly man-marking Portugal dangerman Cristiano Ronaldo!

5

107

Cole is one of only nine players to earn over 100 caps for The Three Lions. His 107 matches put him sixth in the all-time list!

England Legends

KEVIN KEEGAN

Striker

DOB: 14/02/1951

Place of Birth: Doncaster

Strongest Foot: Right

Main Club: Liverpool

England Caps: 63

England Goals: 21

Top Skill: Finishing

Played like... Luis Suarez

Kevin Keegan is the only English player in history to win the Ballon d'Or twice! His mix of top-quality work-rate with mind-blowing skill was a nightmare for defenders to handle and helped him score loads of goals. Keegan started his great career at Scunthorpe, but earned a massive move to Liverpool back in 1971. He formed an unstoppable strike partnership at Anfield with John Toshack and soon helped The Reds become the finest team in England with nine trophies in just six seasons at the club. He helped Liverpool win their first European Cup in his final season at Anfield, then moved to Germany to join Hamburg. He won two Ballon d'Or awards, one Bundesliga title and reached the 1980 European Cup final during his time with the club, before moving back to England to join south coast side Southampton. After his ace playing career, he also became a world-famous manager – helping Newcastle finish runners-up in the 1995-96 Premier League season with an incredible team full of attacking superstars!

HIS GAME RATED!

 Keegan's desire to fight for every single ball was legendary!

 He could score all types of goals, from headers to jaw-dropping volleys!

 He didn't score or play in many major international tournaments for England!

PLAYER STATS

PACE
87

POWER
79

SHOOTING
90

DEFENDING
60

HEADERS
91

SKILL
92

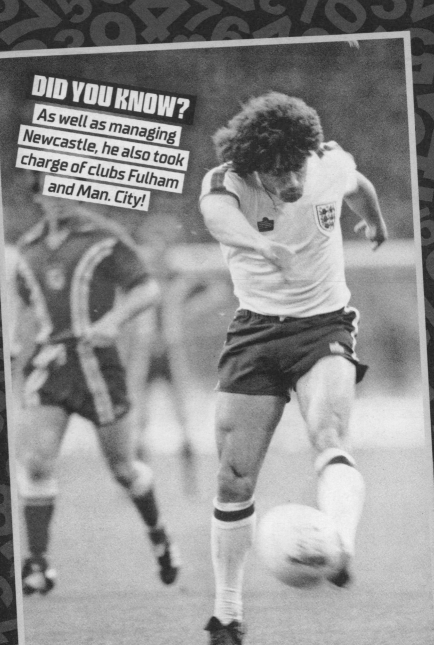

DID YOU KNOW?

As well as managing Newcastle, he also took charge of clubs Fulham and Man. City!

STAT ATTACK!

He scored 48 goals in just 78 league games for Newcastle between 1982 and 1984!

Keegan captained England 31 times, including at two major tournaments – the Euro Championship in 1980 and the 1982 World Cup. Total leader!

He was England manager for 18 games between February 1999 and October 2000. He won seven matches, drew seven and lost four during that time!

Keegan is one of only ten players to win the Ballon d'Or award more than once. He won two during his time at Hamburg in 1978 and 1979. Legend!

His first Three Lions goal came against Wales in 1974. His last strike for his country was v Northern Ireland in 1982!

England Legends

ALAN SHEARER

Striker

DOB: 13/08/1970	**England Caps:** 63
Place of Birth: Gosforth	**England Goals:** 30
Strongest Foot: Right	**Top Skill:** Finishing
Main Club: Newcastle	**Played like...** Harry Kane

Full of power, aggression and an explosive right foot, Alan Shearer was the ultimate striker. He netted vital goals for England v Germany at Euro 2000 and Argentina at the 1998 World Cup, but it was his ace performance at Euro 96 that made him a national icon. England were hosts of the tourno, and Shearer made sure that it was a memorable summer with five excellent goals. He scored in their opening game against Switzerland, then bagged the first goal in a real crunch clash with rivals Scotland. Shearer's best display came in the final group game against the Netherlands – he hit a brace in a 4-1 victory. He went on to give England the lead v Germany in the semi-final to complete an awesome summer and win the Golden Boot with five goals! Modern England hero Harry Kane has been compared loads to Shearer for his ruthless finishing, clever hold-up play and incredible strength – and we can see why. The awesome former Newcastle striker was a total goalscoring hero for both club and country!

HIS GAME RATED!

 Shearer used his footy brain and power to hold up the ball brilliantly!

 His movement and epic finishing inside the box was world-class!

 He should've won more trophies in his wicked net-busting career!

PLAYER STATS

PACE
70

POWER
96

SHOOTING
96

DEFENDING
59

HEADERS
93

SKILL
71

DID YOU KNOW?

Shearer is one of only five players to score five goals in a single Prem game!

11

Shearer has scored the most hat-tricks in Premier League history with 11 trebles! He also won four Prem Player Of The Month awards!

STAT ATTACK!

Alan Shearer is the all-time record goalscorer in Premier League history. He scored 260 goals, which is 52 more than his nearest rival Wayne Rooney!

260

5

He won the Golden Boot at Euro 96 after scoring five goals in five games. Shearer also finished third in the Ballon d'Or vote the same year!

Shearer won three Premier League Golden Boots in a row between 1995 and 1997, including a massive 34-goal total in 1994-95. Awesome!

3

ENGLAND'S
Greatest Ever
MOMENTS!

England were awesome at the 2018 World Cup, but they've had more top moments over the years. Check them out!

KINGS OF THE WORLD!
World Cup 1966

England won their first and only WC trophy in 1966 after an absolutely incredible summer of footy in their own country! The hosts started the tournament with a boring 0-0 draw with Uruguay, but went on to beat Mexico, France, Argentina and then Portugal to reach their first World Cup final. West Germany hit a last-gasp equaliser at Wembley to make it 2-2 in the final, before hero Geoff Hurst bagged a wicked extra-time brace to give The Three Lions a memorable 4-2 win! English footy fans have been speaking about this moment for the last 52 years, and need new heroes!

MOMENT RATING
★ ★ ★ ★ ★

THE TEAM!

Check out the starting XI for England's World Cup final win against West Germany in 1966!

Gordon Banks

George Cohen | Jack Charlton | Bobby Moore | Ray Wilson

Nobby Stiles

Alan Ball | Bobby Charlton | Martin Peters

Geoff Hurst | Roger Hunt

THE GAFFER!
Sir Alf Ramsey

Legendary gaffer Sir Alf Ramsey was England's World Cup-winning boss in 1966. He was a calm and classy manager!

HAT-TRICK HERO!
Sir Geoff Hurst

Will anyone ever follow in Hurst's footsteps and score a hat-trick in a World Cup final? We're not sure anyone will!

THE ROAD TO GLORY!

Group 1

ENGLAND	0-0	URUGUAY

Group 1

ENGLAND	2-0	MEXICO

B. Charlton 37, Hunt 75

Group 1

ENGLAND	2-0	FRANCE

Hunt 38, 75

Quarter-Final

ENGLAND	1-0	ARGENTINA

Hurst 78

Semi-Final

ENGLAND	2-1	PORTUGAL

B. Charlton 30, 80 — Eusebio 82 (p)

Final

ENGLAND	4-2	W. GERMANY

Hurst 18, 101, 120; Peters 78 — Haller 12; Weber 89

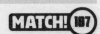

PERFECT PLATT!
World Cup 1990

England were heading towards a penalty shootout in the Last 16 v Belgium at the 1990 WC, before David Platt met Paul Gascoigne's chipped free-kick with a sick volley to send The Three Lions into the quarters. It was in the last minute!

MOMENT RATING
★ ★ ★ ★

GAZZA THE GREAT!
European Championship 1996

We've already mentioned this goal, but it's worth talking about again! England hosted Euro 96 and faced rivals Scotland in the group stage. Step forward Gazza! The England legend helped his country win 2-0 with that outrageous goal!

MOMENT RATING
★ ★ ★ ★

LETHAL LINEKER!
World Cup 1986

Gary Lineker only presents footy nowadays, but he used to be a wicked striker! At the 1986 World Cup, the hitman won the Golden Boot. Half of his six goals arrived in a group stage match against Poland, where he bagged a treble!

MOMENT RATING
★ ★ ★ ★

BRILLIANT BANKS!

World Cup 1970

England went into the 1970 WC as defending champs – and the team to beat. They caused the football world to stand still when they faced Brazil in the group stages – well, legendary goalkeeper Gordon Banks did! He pulled off an epic save from Pele's ace header, and people still say it's the best save today!

MOMENT RATING

★ ★ ★ ★

AWESOME OWEN!

World Cup 1998

Michael Owen became an overnight sporting superstar after he hit one of the best goals in footy history at the 1998 World Cup. He was only 18 at the time, but ran from the centre circle against Argentina with agility and electric pace, then slammed a super shot into the top corner. It was out of this world!

MOMENT RATING

★ ★ ★ ★

DUTCH DESTROYERS!

European Championship 1996

The Netherlands were one of the big faves to win Euro 96, but England humiliated them with a footballing masterclass at Wembley. The Three Lions won 4-1, with doubles from Alan Shearer and Teddy Sheringham. Some fans say it was the greatest display by any England team ever. Wowzers!

MOMENT RATING

★ ★ ★ ★ ★

WICKED WAZZA!

European Championship 2004

Wayne Rooney burst onto the scene at Euro 2004 with a series of epic performances for England. Wazza saved his best for the final group stage match against Croatia, with two goals in a wicked 4-2 win. He became the hottest transfer target on the planet and Man. United won the race!

MOMENT RATING
★ ★ ★ ★

FIVE-STAR LIONS!

World Cup 2002 Qualifiers

England have always had a massive footy rivalry with Germany, so beating them 5-1 in their own stadium in a World Cup qualifier was always going to be special. Net busters from Steven Gerrard and Emile Heskey, plus a wicked Michael Owen hat-trick, sealed an unforgettable win for The Three Lions!

MOMENT RATING
★ ★ ★ ★ ★

QUIZ 2

WHO AM I?

Use the clues to work out the England hero!

→ I won the Prem title in 2017-18!

→ I started my youth career with QPR!

→ I scored 18 Prem goals in 2017-18!

TRUE or FALSE?

Which of these statements are true and which ones are completely made up?

1 Zlatan Ibrahimovic started for Sweden v England in the 2018 WC quarter-final!

2 England's first game at the 2018 World Cup was their sick 6-1 thrashing of Panama!

3 Three of Golden Boot winner Harry Kane's six goals at the 2018 World Cup were pens!

4 Jordan Henderson was the only England player to miss a penalty against Colombia!

5 Jack Butland started in goal for England in their third-place play-off against Belgium!

FIRST XI

Can you answer these 11 rock-hard questions?

1. Five of England's six goals against Panama were from Kane and Stones, but who curled home the other one?

2. How many matches did England lose at the 2018 World Cup – two or three?

3. Which nation hosted Euro 96, when The Three Lions reached the semi-finals?

4. Which former striker won the Golden Boot for England at the 1986 World Cup?

5. What was the last major tourno England didn't qualify for – Euro 2004 or Euro 2008?

6. Which wicked Barcelona superstar scored two goals against England in Group D at the 2014 WC in Brazil?

7. Which club did John Stones join Man. City from in 2016?

8. Which country knocked England out of Euro 2016?

9. Did Harry Kane's penalty v Colombia at WC 2018 come in the second or first half?

10. Who was England gaffer before Gareth Southgate took control back in 2016?

11. Which legend is England's all-time record goalscorer?

QUIZ 2 ANSWERS!

WHO AM I?

Raheem Sterling

TRUE OR FALSE?

1. False
2. False
3. True
4. True
5. False

FIRST XI

1. Jesse Lingard
2. Three
3. England
4. Gary Lineker
5. Euro 2008
6. Luis Suarez
7. Everton
8. Iceland
9. Second-half
10. Sam Allardyce
11. Wayne Rooney

England Future

RYAN SESSEGNON

Left Winger

Club: Fulham	**Strongest Foot:** Left
DOB: 18/05/2000	**Top Skill:** Dribbling
Place of Birth: Roehampton	**Plays like...** Benjamin Mendy
Transfer Value: £40 million	**Pro Debut:** 09/08/2016

Ryan Sessegnon doesn't need to wait a few more years to make a massive impact in footy, because he's already performing at a high level now! The wonderkid really stunned fans in the Championship last season with 16 goals and eight assists as Fulham blasted through the competition to reach the Premier League. His mix of pace, power, dribbling skills and athleticism is incredibly tough to stop, and it'll get even harder the more experienced he becomes. Sessegnon was also a massive part of England's 2017 UEFA European Under-19 Championship success. He scored in the opening game against Bulgaria and also grabbed a double in England's 4-1 win against Germany. This helped Sessegnon finish as the joint-top scorer and be named in the Team Of The Tournament! His Premier League career started in style too, with some wicked performances!

HIS GAME RATED!

 Sessegnon can play in multiple positions, including left-back!

 His pace and dribbling skills can get him past almost any full-back!

 He might need to get stronger to battle the best Prem defenders!

PLAYER STATS

PACE
86

POWER
62

SHOOTING
72

DEFENDING
71

HEADERS
65

SKILL
76

England Future

PHIL FODEN

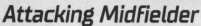

Attacking Midfielder

Club: Man. City	**Strongest Foot:** Left
DOB: 28/05/2000	**Top Skill:** Dribbling
Place of Birth: Stockport	**Plays like...** David Silva
Transfer Value: £25 million	**Pro Debut:** 21/11/2017

England have a lot of exciting wonderkids ready to make a mega impact, but Phil Foden might be top of the tree. The Man. City CAM has already got a Premier League title, FIFA Under-17 World Cup and EFL Cup to his name – and he was only 18 in 2018! His proper classy, creative and skilful performances for England at the FIFA Under-17 World Cup bagged him the Golden Ball for being player of the tourno – an award Toni Kroos won back in 2007. If he can keep learning from Pep Guardiola and the incredible players he trains with every day, he'll only gain more confidence – and one day he might be as good as Germany's World Cup-winning midfield dynamo! Foden started the 2018-19 Prem season as a regular squad player for champions Man. City, and looks ready to gain even more top-level experience in 2019. The England wonderkid has all the tools to become a legend!

HIS GAME RATED!

 Foden dribbles like the ball's stuck to his boots with Super Glue!

 He's an excellent passer and can unlock defences with his wicked vision!

 He's not the strongest, but he's still young so should get tougher!

PLAYER STATS

PACE
74

POWER
51

SHOOTING
61

DEFENDING
50

HEADERS
50

SKILL
86

England Future

JADON SANCHO

Left Winger

Club: Borussia Dortmund	**Strongest Foot:** Right
DOB: 25/03/2000	**Top Skill:** Dribbling
Place of Birth: London	**Plays like...** Raheem Sterling
Transfer Value: £30 million	**Pro Debut:** 21/10/2017

Jadon Sancho has the potential to be a massive star for England at the 2022 World Cup. The ace wing wizard started to pick up loads of hype during his time in the Man. City youth team, then shocked everyone by moving to one of Bundesliga's mega giants – Borussia Dortmund. Not many English footballers move abroad, especially at such a young age, but it's a sign of Sancho's super confidence and maturity that he felt he could do it. He made an instant impact for his new club with some exciting performances off the bench, then truly arrived with a goal and two assists against Bayer Leverkusen in April 2018. He's another youngster to have had success with the Three Lions youth teams, including winning Player Of The Tournament at the 2017 UEFA European Under-17 Championship – and, of course, being in the Team Of The Tourno!

HIS GAME RATED!

 His dribbling and close control are really tough to defend against!

✓ *Sancho is really good at instep finishing, like Tottenham's Harry Kane!*

✗ *He sometimes needs to release the ball to a team-mate earlier!*

PLAYER STATS

PACE
85

POWER
51

SHOOTING
74

DEFENDING
52

HEADERS
52

SKILL
90

MATCH! 183

JOE
GOMEZ

Centre-Back

Club: Liverpool	**Strongest Foot:** Right
DOB: 23/05/1997	**Top Skill:** Power
Place of Birth: London	**Plays like...** Laurent Koscielny
Transfer Value: £35 million	**Pro Debut:** 12/08/2014

Most of England's wonderkids will need time to break into the first-team squad, but Joe Gomez is ready right now. He began the 2018-19 season as a starting CB for Liverpool alongside monster defender Virgil van Dijk, plus he'd already made 23 Premier League apperances the season before. He can play at full-back, but Gomez is most comfortable stopping strikers in their tracks as a centre-back. He has loads of pace for recoveries and awesome strength, but what is most impressive with Gomez is how well he reads the game. The majority of young defenders need years to develop a top footy brain and read strikers' movements, but Gomez struts around Anfield like he's been playing at the top level for years! Don't be too surprised if he's in the starting line-up for The Three Lions' first match of Euro 2020, because the Liverpool hero is more than capable of it. Beast!

HIS GAME RATED!

 Gomez has already got bags of Prem experience playing next to Van Dijk!

 He times his tackles to perfection and rarely gives away fouls!

 He needs to play more big games to get used to mega occasions!

PLAYER STATS

PACE
77

POWER
85

SHOOTING
52

DEFENDING
80

HEADERS
76

SKILL
63

ADEMOLA LOOKMAN

Left Winger

Club: Everton	**Strongest Foot:** Right
DOB: 20/10/1997	**Top Skill:** Pace
Place of Birth: Wandsworth	**Plays like...** Leroy Sane
Transfer Value: £20 million	**Pro Debut:** 03/11/2015

Ademola Lookman has had such an exciting career already – and there's still so much more to come! The electric winger started his career at Charlton and stunned The Valley week after week with his incredible pace and ability to blast in wondergoals with both feet. Everton soon came calling from the Premier League and he started really well, but then his young career took an unexpected twist with a shock loan move to new Bundesliga superclub Red Bull Leipzig. Lookman wowed the German fans with five goals and three assists in just seven league starts. He was also a major part of England's winning team at the 2017 FIFA Under-20 World Cup and scored three net-busters in the knockout stages, including a double against Costa Rica in the Last 16 and a strike against Italy in the semis. His pace will damage defenders for the next ten years!

HIS GAME RATED!

 Lookman's ability to shoot with both feet is a massive weapon!

He has elite close control, slick dribbling skills and lightning-quick pace!

 He can go missing in games and needs to find consistency!

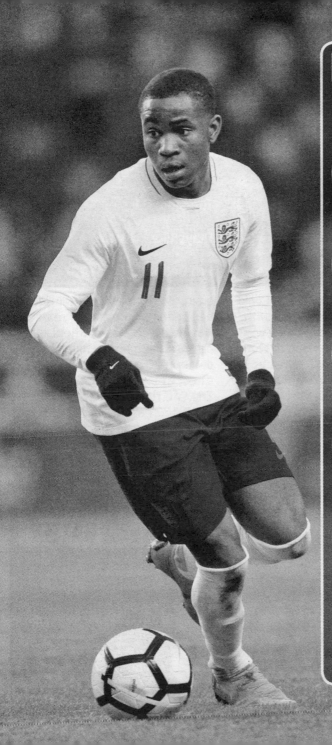

PLAYER STATS

PACE
86

POWER
59

SHOOTING
67

DEFENDING
52

HEADERS
58

SKILL
87

England Future

LEWIS COOK

Central Midfielder

Club: Bournemouth	**Strongest Foot:** Right
DOB: 03/02/1997	**Top Skill:** Passing
Place of Birth: York	**Plays like...** Jorginho
Transfer Value: £15 million	**Pro Debut:** 09/08/2014

Quality midfielder Lewis Cook has something in common with legend Bobby Moore – they've both captained England to World Cup glory! Okay, so Moore's epic triumph was at the main event in 1966, but Cook's heroics at the 2017 FIFA Under-20 World Cup are just as worthy of mega respect. The classy Bournemouth baller has already bagged loads of praise throughout his short career for his leadership skills and footy brain. Most fans would think Cook had been playing for 15 years the way he dominates midfield, but he only made his Premier League debut in 2016. Cook started his career at Leeds, before joining The Cherries at the start of the 2016-17 season. He played six league games in his debut season, but became a regular in 2017-18 with 29 Prem appearances. He made his England debut in 2018 too, and there's more to come!

HIS GAME RATED!

✓ Cook is a classic box-to-box midfielder with bags of energy. He's tireless!

✓ He's a good dribbler and can pick team-mates out with wicked passes!

✗ Cook could become the ultimate midfielder if he improves his shooting!

PLAYER STATS

PACE
67

POWER
78

SHOOTING
60

DEFENDING
75

HEADERS
76

SKILL
77

RHIAN BREWSTER

Striker

Club: Liverpool	**Strongest Foot:** Right
DOB: 01/04/2000	**Top Skill:** Finishing
Place of Birth: London	**Plays like...** Sergio Aguero
Transfer Value: £15 million	**Pro Debut:** N/A

Liverpool and England fans have well high hopes for Rhian Brewster after stunning footy fans, scouts, coaches and experts with classy performances in his youth career. The teenage sensation was the top scorer with eight goals at the 2017 FIFA Under-17 World Cup, which helped England win the epic tournament. He only scored one goal in the group stages, but saved his best performances for the games in the knockout phase, so he obviously enjoys playing on big occasions. He started with a super hat-trick against the United States in the quarter-finals, then smashed home another hat-trick in the semis against the mighty Brazil! Brewster saved one last goal for the final against Spain, and looks set to be a great star in the future! Loads of top young strikers boast pace and dribbling skills, but Brewster combines them with sick movement and finishing!

HIS GAME RATED!

 His pace gets him into loads of really deadly one-on-one situations!

 His technique over a dead ball is awesome, especially free-kicks!

 He needs to be more consistent to break into Liverpool's first team!

PLAYER STATS

PACE
86

POWER
70

SHOOTING
77

DEFENDING
51

HEADERS
69

SKILL
78

England Future

DEMARAI GRAY

Left Winger

Club: Leicester	**Strongest Foot:** Right
DOB: 28/06/1996	**Top Skill:** Dribbling
Place of Birth: Birmingham	**Plays like...** Wilfried Zaha
Transfer Value: £25 million	**Pro Debut:** 01/10/2013

Demarai Gray can leave viewers speechless and full-backs begging for mercy with his incredible wing play! The rapid Leicester star has been compared to Crystal Palace skill machine Wilfried Zaha for his devastating dribbling tekkers and ability to beat any defender with a trick or clever turn. Gray started his career with Birmingham and rapidly turned into a hero at St. Andrew's. He picked up The Blues' Young Player Of The Season and Goal Of The Season awards at the end of the 2014-15 season, aged just 18 at the time. Premier League scouts were watching him most matches and he eventually moved to Leicester in January 2016 – for less than £5 million. Gray couldn't have timed his move to The Foxes any better, because five months later he was collecting an ace Prem winners' medal. He began 2018-19 in great form too, getting his first call-up to the senior England team!

HIS GAME RATED!

 His ability with both feet means he can play on the left and right wing!

 Gray's pace and dribbling are incredible. He's a real nightmare for defenders!

 His finishing needs to improve big-time if he's gonna be a megastar!

PLAYER STATS

PACE
88

POWER
71

SHOOTING
62

DEFENDING
53

HEADERS
57

SKILL
90

England Future

AINSLEY MAITLAND-NILES

Central Midfielder

Club: Arsenal	**Strongest Foot:** Right
DOB: 29/08/1997	**Top Skill:** Power
Place of Birth: London	**Plays like...** Fernandinho
Transfer Value: £15 million	**Pro Debut:** 09/12/2014

It's really tough to break into the first-team squad of a top six club in the Premier League, but that's exactly what star Ainsley Maitland-Niles has managed at Arsenal. The young gun earned Arsene Wenger's respect and the former Gunners gaffer handed him his debut in a central midfield role. Both Wenger and new boss Unai Emery have been impressed with AMN's ability to play in loads of positions, which has resulted in the young Arsenal wonderkid also playing some games at full-back. AMN is a team player who will line up anywhere on the pitch, but his future looks brightest as a central midfielder. His super strength and powerful running style could make him an unstoppable box-to-box CM hero for years to come! When he's on top form and full of confidence, Maitland-Niles doesn't look out of place in the Premier League at all – and he'll only get better!

HIS GAME RATED!

 He bursts away from opponents like Yaya Toure did in his prime!

✓ *His defensive ability and footy brain help him break up attacks!*

 AMN will need to improve his shooting to become a massive midfield star!

PLAYER STATS

PACE
76

POWER
86

SHOOTING
58

DEFENDING
74

HEADERS
69

SKILL
70

England Future

MASON MOUNT

Central Midfielder

Club: Derby (Loan)

DOB: 10/01/1999

Place of Birth: Portsmouth

Transfer Value: £15 million

Strongest Foot: Right

Top Skill: Long shots

Plays like... Aaron Ramsey

Pro Debut: 26/08/2017

Mason Mount has already had a crazier career than some seasoned professionals! Mount grew up in Chelsea's youth team and won back-to-back FA Youth Cups with The Blues in 2015-16 and 2016-17, before completing a surprise loan move to Dutch team Vitesse. The Eredivisie club wanted to keep the wonderkid forever after he had an awesome season for them. Mount was named Vitesse's Player Of The Season after busting 14 nets and grabbing nine assists in just 25 league starts, including his first career hat-trick in a 5-2 away win at ADO Den Haag. Mount was sent out on loan once more at the start of the 2018-19 season, this time to Championship side Derby. New Rams gaffer Frank Lampard was really excited by the loan move, and Mount proved he was worth the hype with a goal on his debut against Reading. His long-range shooting skills are top class!

HIS GAME RATED!

 He hits awesome long shots, just like his boss Frank Lampard used to!

 Mount runs through midfield with bags of confidence and energy!

 He needs to work on the defensive part of his midfield game!

PLAYER STATS

PACE
70

POWER
64

SHOOTING
71

DEFENDING
63

HEADERS
62

SKILL
75

QUIZ 3

WHO STARTED WHERE?

Match the stars with the clubs they started at!

ERIC DIER

1

DELE ALLI

2

ASHLEY YOUNG

3

HARRY MAGUIRE

4

A SHEFFIELD UNITED

B SPORTING

C WATFORD

D MK DONS

 MATCH!

TRANSFER TRACKER!

Fill in the missing club that defender Gary Cahill has played for!

2004-2008
Aston Villa

2004-2005
Burnley (Loan)

2007-2008
Sheff. United (Loan)

2008-2012
?

2012-
Chelsea

WORDSEARCH

Can you find 20 England WC 2018 stars in this mega grid?

- Alli
- Butland
- Cahill
- Delph
- Dier
- Henderson
- Jones
- Kane
- Lingard
- Maguire

- Pickford
- Rashford
- Rose
- Sterling
- Stones
- Trippier
- Vardy
- Walker
- Welbeck
- Young

Pick your...
EURO 2020 DREAM TEAM

Write your England team for Euro 2020!

GK

CB

CB

RB

LB

CM

CM

AM

AM

AM

ST